FOUR CONVERSATIONS ON THE
ARCHITECTURE OF DISCOURSE

Aaron Levy and William Menking

Four Conversations on the Architecture of Discourse

ARCHITECTURAL ASSOCIATION LONDON

Contents

Introduction

Aaron Levy

Architecture on Display is a two-part research initiative and series of publications that explores the vexed relationship between architecture and its publics, uniting around a simple premise: that architecture problematises its own display.

The initiative began with a series of interviews that Bill Menking and I conducted with the former directors of the Venice Biennale of Architecture, which, since 1980, has become the most internationally prestigious venue for the display of architecture. Those interviews, also published by the AA, recover the forgotten history of this exhibition and explore its indebtedness to the social and political movements of the late 1960s. Our questions were informed by our experience at the 2008 Venice Biennale, when *Into the Open*, our installation for the US pavilion, was arguably overshadowed by economic, political and touristic tensions – tensions that Venice does not have the monopoly on, but have come to define contemporary curating in general. The findings that emerged from those interviews, together with a new generation's interest in questioning architecture on display, acted as the catalyst for the second part of this project, in which we move beyond the biennial spotlight on the lagoon of Venice to foreground other critical positions.

We brought together five institutions – the Architectural Association, Dark Side Club, Graham Foundation, Slought Foundation and Storefront for Art and Architecture – to collaborate with us on the conversations that follow. The invited participants reflect a variety of disciplinary and institutional perspectives, and include architects and designers, theorists and historians, editors and publishers, directors and funders, and students and professors.

These transcripts elucidate the relation of architecture to display and highlight certain themes, such as the importance of cultivating critical and creative publics and the way in which exhibitions can function as active agents for innovation and change. They also provide the reader with critical perspectives that help mitigate the paucity of contemporary discourse on architectural display.

While the first of these publications consisted of interviews, this second volume assumes a dialogic approach that reflects the process of refining and rethinking one's practice on an ongoing basis and in discussion with others. For this reason, the voices featured within this book do not always establish their own authoritative vector, or formalise themselves as particularly oppositional. Instead, the many views construct, with self-reflection and openness, a poetics of agreement. If there is urgency to this dialogic approach, it is because the histories and terminologies that are regularly invoked in contemporary architectural discourse – for instance, between those advocating social engagement and those championing the parametric – often seem irreconcilable. What emerges throughout these conversations is a concern for the plurality of definitions at play, as well as an acknowledgement of the productive nature of disagreement. In this respect, the book may be approached as a series of open scores in which live dialogues are performed before the reader as models for continued conversation.

Insofar as these conversations took place in cultural spaces, the architectural surroundings contributed to transforming the nature of each discussion, and solicited expectations more readily associated with an informal event. With this publication, we hope to also convey a sense of immediacy that approximates participation in the conversations themselves – and to raise questions about how certain forms of practice and discourse are typically reproduced.

By placing these conversations not in the institutional repository but rather in the public domain, we hope they may enable new forms of practice to emerge and serve as a starting point for continued discussion concerning architectures of display. Furthermore, in structuring this publication around a series of open-ended conversations, rather than commissioned positions or edited statements, we have also made a conscious decision to critique the notion that curating is a specialised discourse or a passive staging of existing knowledge. We thus invite you to continue the conversation in your own home, community and places of work, and with colleagues, friends and strangers.

*   *   *

This project is a Slought Foundation 2010–11 research initiative. Accordingly, we would like to thank Megan Schmidgal, research fellow Clare Kobasa, and curatorial fellow Andreea Bailuc, each of whom assisted with the organisation of the events and their preparation for publication. The featured conversations were made possible through the collaboration of Robert White of the Dark Side Club; Eva Franch i Gilabert of the Storefront for Art and Architecture; Brett Steele and Roberta Jenkins of the AA School; and Sarah Herda and Ellen Hartwell Alderman of the Graham Foundation. We would also like to thank the AA Print Studio for editing these documents for publication.
Finally, we wish to thank the many participants in these dialogues. Their willingness to enter into conversation with us, often without knowing where these conversations would lead, is admirable.

They have helped us think anew about architecture on display and how we can each, in our respective practices, work towards cultivating publics who are critical and creative.

New

Venice

Chic

York

London

:ago

Conversation One
Venice

Dark Side Club, Venice

This conversation took place on 28 August 2010. It was organised by Aaron Levy, William Menking and Robert White.

Aaron Betsky: I think that the question of the public is a very interesting place to begin, because the Venice Biennale – whether it's the art or the architecture biennale, or the film, theatre or dance festival – is first and foremost a gathering of a tribe. And it would be interesting to look at when, historically, its main purpose changed from being a display of national prowess to being a gathering of a tribe of the people who produce that prowess. In other words, the biennale started as a way for Italy to show that it too was still producing things, and for all the participating countries to show what they could do in the highest sphere of human creativity, which was art. At a certain point it became a place where people who made art, or who bought and sold it, would come together to see what everyone else was doing.

From the perspective of someone who has tried to be a curator, I would say that curating a

15

biennale is much like directing a museum, in that the reason behind both is to bring people and architecture together. This means you have to find a way of making architecture present and making people present. You can't just point to architecture that exists elsewhere, showing buildings only through models, photographs or drawings; instead, the architecture has to be present in such a way that people will notice it, want to understand more about it, become part of a relationship with it – and hopefully in a social way. If this all sounds simplistic, it's intentional. I think that Kazuyo Sejima has pursued this issue successfully in making forms that through their presence (though I hate this word) 'engage' a public, are visually and formally attractive, and have a way of eliciting responses. This is, to me, the crucial question: how do you do this?

William Menking: And you feel that Sejima's biennale does this successfully?

AB: As someone who is just looking at the biennale now, rather than directing it, I think there are many contributions that are effective. And the effect is all I care about, very simply. When architects try to explain what they are doing – and maybe I can get Tony or Odile or Francine or someone to fight with me – I want them to shut up. They make the architecture and I explain what it's about. I like to joke that, as a failed architect, I had to find something else to do – and this is what I do, and in a certain sense it's what a biennale tries to do. It tries to bring together architects who do things, and to explain what they're doing in such a way that a public begins to connect with it.

Odile Decq: I don't understand why curators hate architects and architecture. I have the impression that we don't actually talk about architecture. Everybody talks about themselves without talking to the public or trying to do something more, push things further. Instead, they are just playing and showing off.

Sam Chermayeff: I think the important question here is: what is it that makes the biennale meaningful? On the whole, it seems to be the rhythm of the exhibition that makes it good, some kind of tone that moves across the whole thing. Working with Sejima, I spent a long time looking into each person's proposal, and sending thousands of little emails saying 'Move this around', 'Are you sureyou want to do it like that?', 'Let's get a video monitor here', and so on and so forth. But the value of the whole thing is not in these details, but in the fact that it goes from heavy to light, open to closed, then dark. There's a nice flow, a kind of musical rhythm constructed for the public.

Aaron Levy: We asked Paolo Baratta, the current president of the Venice Biennale, to talk about what Paolo Portoghesi's architecture biennale and Strada Novissima meant to him. He argued that one has to be bold and cinematic and theatrical – that if a curator is made anxious by the scale of the Arsenale, then they should go do something else. And it was, for us, a really interesting moment that crystallised the disparity between how he thinks about curation and our view of it, because frankly we're uncomfortable with spectacle, scale and the more theatrical aspects of contemporary installations.

AB: When Baratta asked me what a biennale would be, I said, 'First of all, you have to understand that it's a spectacle.' A biennale is an opportunity, if you're lucky, for serious discussion and all kinds of other things to happen. But the central event in the Arsenale and in what used to be the Italian pavilion, and is now the Pavilion of Expositions, is a spectacle…

OD: It's entertainment.

AB: No, it's not entertainment – spectacle is a different thing. And by the way, I found it very offensive that you say that we hate architects. I hate architects who are obnoxious, and self-righteous and full of themselves. But I don't think any of us would be in this if we didn't love architects, and love architecture, and admire architects and want them to do the most incredible things.

OD: So you ask architects to pretend to be artists.

AB: I ask architects to pretend to be architects.

OD: So architects pretend to be artists too?

AB: No, they make architecture.

OD: No, they pretend to be artists.

WM: Let's ask Tony, as he's also an architect.

AB: You collaborate with an artist, but I don't think you pretend to be an artist. You have no desire to pretend to be an artist, do you?

Tony Fretton: No, but my exhibition is very different from making architecture. It's not about being an artist, but is about doing something different from what you usually do.

WM: How is that? Are you concerned about the public, for instance, in a way that's different from when you're doing architecture?

TF: Well, in the end, I think that we have appealed to an architectural public rather than the general public. And that's a very different position from making an exhibition that presents architecture to a public that isn't engaged in architecture – which is probably the proposition of the biennale. What will happen, I think, is that this will devolve into a situation where architects present architectural ideas to a public that they hope is interested. Anything beyond this and you'd have to have rather more dictatorial control by the director, a much longer lead time and many more internal discussions – none of which are available because of the way the biennale has been constructed.

> SC: Tony, I disagree with you: you don't understand your projects at all! It's a great installation. You walk in there and feel all kinds of things, but you don't take from it a particular idea about architecture. It's like a tone, or a feeling that you experience – something like the sensibility of an artist. In that way, it's no different at all from an art biennale.

TF: But art and architecture are very different. Having worked as an architect with artists, it's a different proposition. If you're presenting in the biennale as an architect – if you're making an architectural presentation – it's very leaden. You have to modify the material in order that you can look at it in an exhibition. You have to select it, reduce it; you have to make something that people can understand in quite a short time.

SC: But wouldn't you say, then, that it's art?

TF: Well, to put it crudely, I think it's about exhibition design, which is a different field of design, but it's design rather than art. It's about design in the sense that it's about communication with people. If it's art, you can do anything you want; if it's architecture, it has to please somebody.

AB: All I can do is smile, because for me it's so useless to debate whether it's art or architecture. You engage in work that uses a particular discipline to create objects and/or images that have a physical reality and, if they're good, have not only an internal consistency but also a critical relationship to our society. For me, it doesn't matter at all what the particular discipline is, as long as the work follows its discipline with clarity and great competence. What's more important is that there is a series of crucial issues that we as human beings have to confront. When, as curator, you choose a series of topics – when Ricky Burdett chooses a series of issues about urban growth and how we inhabit the city, when you, Sam, talk with Sejima about how we meet and create relationships within

21

our social fabric – the basis on which the work should be criticised is not whether it's art, or architecture, or puff pastry, but whether it responds to that theme. We were talking in my biennale about utopia or experimental architecture. This, for me, is a more interesting and crucial divide. Do you believe in utopia, do you believe in experimental architecture or do you believe in whatever position you want to take? This is much more interesting than whether it is made by Olafur Eliasson, Odile Decq or Tony Fretton.

Eva Franch i Gilabert: Talking about the distinction between art and architecture, and why that distinction is something that keeps on coming up, wouldn't you agree that every time an architect uses the excuse of going into art, it's because architecture has a disciplinary specificity that is always being defied?

AB: So does art, visually; so do painting and sculpture.

EFG: But the essence of art is its constant redefinition. So the moment that architecture wants to redefine itself, it moves into art. That's why the pairing of art and architecture is desirable, not as an excuse but as a vector of moving towards something else. Coming back to this biennale and what we have seen these last few days, there were some projects that were objects of display of a certain anachronistic thought or personal agenda, some projects that were trying to be performative, some that were trying to engage the public either through empathy or notions of effect, and others that were trying to go beyond notions of communication towards notions of sensation. And perhaps there were some other moments that were even more provocative.

AB: More didactic …

EFG: Didactic, or agitators. We could say that the question of 'What is display?' is found in the OMA project about preservation, which is really pedagogical and clearly trying to engage with that. So the idea of a distinction between these three aspects – the one that is displaying an ideology, the one that is trying to perform an action of engagement and the one that is trying to teach a moment of dialogical exchange – has been orchestrated through asking an interesting question. What is most important is that there is this variety within the biennale. I'm really happy with both the successful pavilions and the really terrible pieces that I saw, because I think it's important to feel repulsion towards certain elements, to feel that they are unacceptable.

AB: It's brilliant what you said. Perhaps there is also a fourth perspective to be had, which is maybe what Odile is trying to get at with her notion of art: some things try to escape, or bring silence, or bring nothingness. But you're right: these are much more crucial distinctions than whether something is art or architecture or anything else.

EFG: We've just learned who has won some of the biennale awards. After talking to several people I think we need to discuss the winning national pavilion – Bahrain's – and ask why it won. It is trying to raise a series of questions. It is probably about a combination of the three things I mentioned before. Firstly, it is displaying a sociopolitical and environmental condition. It is also engaging in a moment of performance – you go there, sit there, feel the atmosphere, and there is a kind of friendship. At the same time it is pedagogical, in the sense of trying to teach you about notions like ownership, property, borders, politics and so on. So I think it is successful because it is actually engaging with these three aspects. The other pavilions are just doing one single thing, and this one is actually doing these three things at the same time.

WM: I don't want to ask Beatriz to speak for the jurors, but do you want to say anything…

Beatriz Colomina: No, I couldn't, and I also think that what actually wins in terms of prizes is not all that important. What really matters is what the architectural community decides is important, what touches you in some way.

Concerning the biennale in general, countries that really should know better after all these years still treat their pavilions like real estate. I mean, they present you with all the latest developments by their star architects: 'Here we have this', 'These are the great architects'. But do we need to see pieces that we have already seen in the press or in the media? It's extraordinary how they can still get away with this.

Bahrain could have done the same thing but instead made a courageous choice to do some kind of self-analysis of what is happening. As Eva was saying, it presents very clearly the situation of this coastline in a country that has traditionally had a relationship to the sea but is now in a phase of increasing urbanisation, of the kind you can find anywhere else in the world. And by making the choice of bringing this hut to Venice, they are raising the question of reclaiming – the word 'reclaim' is important – the sea as a form of public space. I don't know whether it happened to you, but I was passing through the Arsenale, already exhausted with all these things you have to see, and I came to this exhibition and it's a very optimistic project.

OD: I sat down and I had a conversation with one of the guys from there.

BC: You sit down, and you have something of a conversation. They're incredibly kind, and I was not yet thinking critically. I was thinking that maybe this is like a World's Fair, and this is a reproduction of a fisherman's house. I was a little bit suspicious and thought maybe this is just a little bit kitsch. But when I understood what is happening in this pavilion – through watching the films and talking to them – I realised that it is critical of the situation. So a very strong message is communicated to you in this kind of domestic setting. You understand the conditions of life there, and in that sense you learn something. And I also think it is a very good pavilion to represent what Sejima has tried to do in this biennale: asking how people meet in architecture.

WM: It really speaks to the public, don't you think?

BC: Yes, but it's not just that. I don't know what your experience was, but as I said, you pass through all these pavilions and this is the one you immediately sit down in. You have this screen, and there's always somebody around. There's a woman with a scarf, they often have some dates, there's some tea. And then all of a sudden you're transported to another world, and you understand that reality in a much more immediate way than if there were lots of planners telling you how many buildings they had built, or the statistics of this and that, which is a much more abstract form, and which would have been closer to what Ricky Burdett did, or what other biennales tried to do. And I think in that sense, this pavilion captures the spirit of this biennale.

Abaseh Mirvali: I also think it's interesting, and I spoke with them as well. I'm Iranian, of American and Iranian heritage, and Bahrain belonged to Iran at a certain point, so we were engaging in a cultural conversation. It's the first time that I have seen one of the countries from the region – particularly after the spectacularly unsuccessful demonstration by the United Arab Emirates – actually present real conditions. They didn't have to pretend to be something that they're not.

Aaron Levy: Matteo, I was wondering if you wanted to add your voice to the mix. You played a crucial role in Kurt Forster's biennale, so you are observing these developments with a few years' distance, and looking back on the institution from an insider's perspective. Perhaps it looks like the same kind of space you were working in back then, marked by the same kinds of tensions?

Matteo Cainer: Yes, it has been six years now. One of the issues that is important to me is, who are you really doing the biennale for? People come, students and everyone else, to be inspired by the biennale. They expect to see architecture as a kind of seismograph of where we are. When I walk through the biennale today, I ask myself if I might be conscious of where we are now, what is the message that actually comes out? It is a question of sensation. When we did our biennale, we divided the world hypothetically into various sections: a section for atmosphere, for sensation, etc. Six years on, I see that the biennale is again about the question of sensation and how you feel in space. Is this really a sign of the times, of where architecture is right now?

This has happened in other biennales too, but Sam [Chermayeff], you're giving the architect the role of being a curator of his own piece, instead of actually curating and deciding a line of thought. And if I can attach myself to what Odile was saying: who's talking, is it the architect or is it the curator? The minute that you make a piece of work, is it because the director asked you to give the sensation or is it because this is what you're feeling? It's as if we're talking among ourselves and saying, 'I did this, you did this, this is great' – and it's all a kind of reflection on yourself. Instead, we should be discussing where architecture is going, what are the fundamental problematics right now.

Yael Reisner: For me, this biennale is not about architecture, it's about something else. I always judge it first as an architect: I should be surprised, enlightened and excited. But for me that experience was missing. The part that I saw of the Arsenale, which I know is in the control of Sejima, feels old-fashioned. The first work I saw, as I entered from the main entrance, looked like it was made by an artist. And I thought, 'Why?'

OD: OK, I agree that it's mainly architects and students who are coming. The larger public? Not so much. But even if it's not for the larger public, they still want to know what we're doing. Because it is a question of what is architecture. And this is an important question: what are the real questions of architecture, today and tomorrow? The biennale is not only for talking about ourselves; it's for talking about what we're working on, and for whom. And we are not just making art, you know. This is why I ask this question: why do you hate architects so much?

AB: Maybe it's only when architects fail that I hate them.

OD: No, it's just some sort of metaphor.

EFG: No, that's a mistake, failure is underrated. Failure is important, in all kinds of research, in scientific research, in architecture …

AB: You're right. I'll adjust that, only when architects lie …

EFG: Lying is something else, but failure …

AB: Yes this is something different, I agree. I apologise.

EFG: With success, you don't really learn much. But when you fail at something, then you learn something.

AB: Lying is another issue.

AL: Brett, were you trying to offer another vantage point on architecture and the biennale by locating the AA's activities at the Fondazione Cini, on the island of San Giorgio Maggiore? Is there something you are trying to say about architecture's vexed relationship with its public?

Brett Steele: Architecture has a fundamental and deep-rooted problem with the idea of having an audience, to the point that this conversation was rehearsed almost 100 years ago, when the founders of what we think of as modern architecture today were curators and certainly not builders. People like Mies or Corb, for example, either as editors or curators learned to invent an idea of modern architecture long before they went on to build it. The idea that architecture remains trapped in that kind of a dichotomy is a striking record of this difficulty we have with audience.

I was asked in an interview earlier today how many people this biennale is for, and I struggled to come up with a number. There are 100–200 people around the world who I think need to see it to understand where the impulse is. There is a very small group of people here, but I think architecture over several decades has mastered that form of discussion. What we struggle with – and I think there are other fields doing it incredibly well today – is that other category of audience that registers at an exponential kind of scale. Two nights ago, at the Fondazione Cini, I was thinking all we really need is cable TV so that thousands of people over in the garden could follow the conversation. But we don't have that.

YR: How many times do you see any exposure of architecture in the media?

BS: I'm not talking about the mediatisation so much as how an event like this, which is measured by people on the ground, always has a fairly stable size. We all come to this every two years, and it's roughly the same size and crowd. How can it grow exponentially? And that's the demand I think we really should place on it. The numbers for the Frieze art fair are staggering. To see it set up in one year and have a few thousand people, the next year to have maybe up to ten thousand, a year later a hundred thousand and the year after that a quarter million? And there are other fields, not far from ours, that are demonstrating an ability to do that as well. I'm talking to publishers right now who are genuinely perplexed as to why architecture can't publish more books.

OD: But excuse me, this is not a question of numbers. This is not about the fact that thousands of people are coming. It's a question of quality first.

BS: No, but it's one way of measuring our engagement with the world. I would argue that the quality's there, Odile. I would say that the 100 or 200 people who need to see the show are affected in various ways and form opinions of what works and what doesn't work. But it would be nice for a couple of hundred thousand other people to do it. There just ain't enough people here! It isn't a big enough discussion, and it isn't a big enough public.

EFG: But there is a difference between cultural consumption and cultural production. And I think that's what you are trying to target. That's the differentiation between modes of communication and modes of engagement. And we don't want to be equated with any film festival. If the Biennale of Architecture can have any strength, it's not because of its ability to be branded, but as a practice.

BS: I meant it more as an imperative: the communicative imperative for architects to reach out to audiences at a scale that simply goes way beyond what we're currently comfortable with. I think we do it well at a scale we like. But films moved here in 1932, within months of the invention of this medium, and as an expression of that medium's interest in a larger audience and public. That's all I'm saying. Architecture might want to recover more. I want another million people.

YR: But I brought up the topic of media exposure only as an indication of the lack of interest in us.

BS: What the publishers are struggling over is how a field like economics has such a wide appeal. For example, you get someone like Stieglitz writing to his 64 peers around the world and doing it brilliantly. But then he finds a way to communicate to several hundred thousand in a different form, in a different way. I think architects have that ability. I think they've had it before, it's just that we're at a

very interesting moment now where we don't
seem to have that kind of dual channel capacity.

Peter Cook: There's a hunger and there's a machine.
If you go to the blogs, if you talk with the younger
people who work with you, there's an enormous
hunger. When I get back to London in two days'
time they'll be saying, 'OK, what was there, what
was happening, what did people say?'
    And the machine, by which I mean the
biennale as it stands, is a funny cranky machine.
It has these national pavilions, and each time it
has somebody who sets up a theme. Now, most
of us know that people who want to show in the
exhibition ignore the machine and say, 'Oh the
theme is this – business as usual.' I think that the
theme ought to be talent, that's my view. This is
my sixth or seventh biennale. If you love it, it's the
best networking operation. It saves a lot of time
to come here and bump into everybody. But the
network operates irrespective, and that's terrible.
There's a lot of talent out there. The filter through
which that talent gets on the wall, or on the table
or on the video in the exhibition, is patronage.
One year you're a patron, another year I'm a patron.
But that's still a creaking thing, and the best things
in the last three or four biennales have been those
you've almost missed: you know, you're nearly
getting onto the plane and someone says, 'You
ought to go around to the Hungarian – or the

Canadian or Belgian – pavilion, it's not so bad.'
Because the old warhorses – the US and British
pavilions – have such a long-winded filtration
system that by the time people get up on the wall,
you've been talking about them for 20 years.
And I was up once, so I know.

It is wonderful to come here, but I have a
horrible feeling that if it goes on like this another
two or three cycles, somebody else will invent
something else, just as blogs have reinvented
magazines. And I like coming here too. I like sitting
outside the Florian and having a latte, and wearing
my straw hat. But sooner or later that will die. And
it's not good enough, because I think those of us
sitting around here have a passion for architecture.
Even if I think Tony Fretton is boring as hell, I'm
glad he's there! Somehow one knows instinctively,
over five, six, or seven biennales, that it's losing it.
We'll still come here because it saves a lot of time
meeting people, but that should not be the reason.

> OD: We want to enjoy, to look at something
> that is fresh, unexpected, that you are surprised
> by. That's all. But we are not surprised by what
> we see, and that's the problem. We just think,
> 'This is another thing like that', or 'We already
> saw a thing like that in an art fair'.

BS: Fair enough, but you have to remember that
there is a generation that is surprised. The fact is

that you, me and many in this room spend most of the year travelling around the world, seeing all the work that's reconfigured into a show like this. I think there still is genuine excitement among a generation of kids who haven't seen this stuff. And there is a reason why that crowd comes here, but what I can't come up with is a mechanism to explain why anyone other than an architect would come here. And I think we have to do that.

AB: Do you want statistics? The reality is that at both the art and architecture biennale when they do surveys, less than half the people are in some way affiliated with art and architecture, either as students or as one of us. At the art biennale, 400,000 come. At the architecture biennale, 200,000 come. Now, we can do the usual guilt of the avant-garde elite wealthy intellectuals and say, 'We're only talking to ourselves, how horrible, we only talk to our students!' Or, 'Oh my God, I'm so bored, I must be amused by something new.' Or, 'I'm going to die of boredom.' Or instead we can say, 'Look, with all we know how to do and all we think is important, we must contribute our skills and knowledge to figure out what we can contribute to issues that are of great importance.' Whether they are issues of sprawl, the misuse of our environment or the destruction of liberties, we need to ask what we, as architects, can do about them. And what we can do about them with our buildings and with forms, spaces and images. That is what a biennale should do: it should try to engage as many people as possible while understanding its limitations, both of form and audience.

EFG: I think that's true, but there's one thing that's missing, namely the possibility of framing a question that goes beyond your own cultural, social and disciplinary expertise. Think of Bahrain – you would never have been able to ask a question that would have triggered that exhibition as an answer. How do you actually frame a biennale or a space of conversation so that certain global desires, human values and commonalities are responded to in a local manner? So, I think you are right, but you can fall into the trap of imposing certain constraints that can be constraining ideologically.

AB: Always a danger. But that is why I would disagree with Sam [Chermayeff], when he says that as curator you only set a tone. Because I think that the orchestration is critical. Orchestration is like urban planning. It's not about telling people what to see or think, but about how you get people to look and see, and allow completely unpredictable things to happen. I tried to pose what I thought was a simple yet complex question, which started from what

I think of as architecture, and to turn it into a big question. Given that our world is more and more controlled by systems that we see as being outside our control – political, economic and technological systems – how can we use the particular expertise of architecture to reveal those systems as they manifest themselves in the physical reality we inhabit? And how can we do this in such a way that we can take hold of and appropriate them, and make a place of our own within this world?

OD: OK, what you say is really interesting. But what was shown here two years ago was not, excuse me.

AB: Well, then for you it was a failure.

OD: No, it was not a failure, but there were so many installations that were not talking about that. This is the problem. What you said is very interesting, but what was there was not. It's not your fault, it's the fault of the architects maybe …

AB: Well, many critics agreed with you. But this is all I can do as a curator. I think we all choose questions like this, and this is all that the biennale can try to do.

OD: Reject the architect – definitely! It's a joke …

AB: Only if they lie!

WM: You publish, and you are interested in magazines and publications and different forms of introducing architectural ideas. You were going to hold up this new magazine a while ago. What were you trying to get at there?

BS: It wouldn't surprise me if in 20 years' time some group of people is sitting together here discussing what is at stake. They will look back at what happened over the last 20 years, and will examine whether we raised the right issues. Did we reach people? Did we engage people? Not through display, but through the issues. Are we smart enough to identify those issues today, and to specify architecture as the right tool, as the right dimension to think through these issues and to come up with the right result? Maybe we are now at a turning point: at the very end of discussing the display of architecture in terms of strategies. We just need to start anew, raising issues that people really are concerned with, and we need to start trying to connect this discipline in all its specificity.

AB: From that perspective, this biennale makes a good argument for continuing biennales – maybe not for 20 years, but at least for a few more years – exactly because it calls us back to the manipulation of reality. If two or four biennales ago we were stuck in a kind of iPod aesthetic, where everything was honed down and everything was information, now we are beginning to ask the question: how can these issues be raised in a physical location, through spectacle or in any of the categories that you mentioned? And this is because we have found that there is a value to doing it in that mode, as opposed to doing it in a book or magazine. That, for me, is the crucial task of a biennale. I mean the internal task, not the task in terms of a public.

BS: The biennale hasn't been thought of as having a history, since it's only about 30 years old and has had only a dozen or so curators. The idea that a history is now being assembled in Architecture on Display certainly suggests the formalisation of a subject of extended research and study. This makes me think again about the role history has played at various times in the biennales. I thought that Aaron Betsky's selection in his biennale of things like *Roma interrotta*, which he suddenly brought back, was incredibly important. The one great potential that this institution seems to have – and other audience-making instruments don't – is the introduction of a historical component to the things that Aaron is framing here as problems. The people who are coming to the biennale are coming here because it's Venice, not because it's Shanghai. They're coming to a place of deep history. And I think that the idea of using it as an instrument to introduce history back into the biennale, at least to problems that we all want to frame around the crisis of 2010, would be a really great project.

EFG: I want to insist on one thing that Aaron [Betsky] is trying to push. I think it's important to reflect on how many questions architecture, and the biennale, can actually ask. Architecture – starting in 1976 or 78 with the biennale, but also throughout its larger history – has perhaps only asked one very simple question: how do you want to live together? The moment you ask how people should live together, then suddenly there are specific moments and responses which answer political, social, moral and ethical questions that might be raised in a specific local context. And we should not think that architecture has a specificity that is static, because then we would not be architects anymore. That's just a question that I would like to put to you, Aaron, because that's what you're arguing for, right?

Abaseh Mirvali: It's interesting that you all started out by saying that you were going to talk about the problems of displaying architecture. I do think that a lot of the architectural exhibitions ask the right questions, but don't know how to exhibit them. None of you have addressed the question of exhibiting, which is the biggest question. I ran a museum, and the pain of going to architectural shows … Well, they're painful and make you want to cry because you see the work of architects who you adore, and there is all this reading, and you feel nothing. What are you to feel looking at a maquette? What is it supposed to impart to you? Can you transport yourself and see the sensation, feel it, admire that the cabling went this way, or that the air conditioning was piped outside and that saved money? I mean, how do you go through all of that display? None of you have spoken about how to display it properly. At the end of the day, this is not a conference or a PowerPoint presentation. We are supposed to be experiencing, but how, today, do you think we should experience?

Sam Jacob: This is my first time at the biennale, and it's been a strange experience. One of the weirdest things was a quote from Sejima about the fact that we live in a post-ideological age. Which seems a very strange statement. But it also seems the opposite of what people meet in architecture. So I wanted to ask Sam, what's the difference between these two.

SC: Sejima is always forced into these sorts of comments, and if Sejima were left to her

42

own devices she would not say a single word to the press – not a peep. Aaron [Betsky], you have such a nice explanation about what your biennale tried to do. Sejima just tried to choose nice things, and that's it, in the most basic sense.

OD: But this is problematic.

SC: No, not really. Let's go over to the darkest side of all conversations about art and architecture. Why don't we just make it a question of taste? Isn't that really what it comes down to? Sejima decided these things, and they all fit into some idea of what she thinks makes sense.

Mark Wigley: This is a kind of sad conversation. It has the sort of tone of talking about your mother – she being, of course, the source of infinite nightmares. The biennale is never going to be the perfect representation of architecture of the past, or the present, or the future. It's a kind of architectural project. What I admire about this biennale is that Sam and Sejima and the team treated it as a project, and they did their best to steer the details of the project in the line of their thinking. There's a lot of editing going on, it's all about trying to maximise the amount of editing. And sure, in a perfect world there could have been more editing. We don't ask of any project that it fully represent the state of the universe. It represents the struggle between the

43

dreams of the architect and the realities of the situation. And in Venice you could say there are so many realities. How could one possibly imagine that in Venice one could successfully stage a representation of contemporary architecture? So, following Peter's argument, it seems you are asking an architect to make one big project that is, for sure, full of problems. It's almost a kamikaze mission: one in which you are destined to fail. The better you are, the more precise your critics can be, and it enables them – this tribe of architects – to circle around the corpse of this exhibition, complaining. Were there to be an exhibition that, to put it the other way around, fully communicated the world of architecture today, I think everybody in this room would be shocked and beyond belief.

I want to make a hypothesis. If reducing the number of represented architects radically, by about half, made for such a fresh exchange, maybe it has to be halved again, and halved again. In terms of Peter's point about the creaking nature of institutions, it seems we do have to face the kind of perversity of national pavilions in an age of radical globalisation – not because nations have disappeared, but because they have multiplied. There are millions of them now, and all of the countries that are represented are now subdividing into multiple ones; and there are civil wars going on in most of the countries being represented. And on a technological level, there is a huge redundancy in the

44

national pavilion area, which is, not by chance, the area in which the curators have the least control. But Sam, I thought you and Sejima did an amazing job of trying to tame the national pavilions as much as you could. I think Sejima and the gang came through with incredible dignity, a lot of beauty, a lot of intelligence, and we found our surprises.

I refused to come to biennales for years precisely because I thought it was this kind of networking/supermarket situation, in which architecture was vulgarised beyond belief and made, at least for a moment, to look like a commodity. Now I love them all, they're great – they're always bad. Though this one is not as bad as it should have been.

AM: But I hope it's not about cutting more architects. And I don't think adding more artists is the solution either – we have enough art. We really want to see architecture …

Mark Wigley: Hypothetically, if there were ten architects allowed to present at Venice, choosing whatever piece of territory they wanted, boy, would this debate be fierce. If you go to an art biennale, all you see is architecture. So when you see a little bit of art in the architecture one then hey, fair's fair.

Francine Houben: I was the first director and curator of the International Architecture Biennale Rotterdam. I had to do both, and I had three thoughts about it. First, I could not copy Venice. I didn't have the money, and I didn't have such a beautiful city, though I like Rotterdam. For me, Venice was just about famous architects. The second thought was: why do I want to organise a biennale? For me, it was because of the experience I had at the biennale in São Paulo in 2000, which was so much fun. I only remember the ten days that I was building my exhibition with my own team in this beautiful building in this beautiful park in São Paulo, and we were there with all the other architects from other countries, building together and eating local food. Those were the best days, and then at the opening there were all these official people in the building. For us it was over at that point. Our biennale was just those ten days together: famous and young architects from all over the world, and I'm still in contact with them. The third thought was about responsibility. We did it in the Netherlands with public money. I have no idea how it works here in Italy, financially. I felt a sense of responsibility: if I get money from the public, I also want to give back to the public.

I feel that the main problem is not architecture, but all the subjects we have never had in our education. For instance, what is between architecture and urbanism? We have no solutions, abilities or even ideas about what that is. In Rotterdam, I organised a kind of laboratory of ideas, and it was also fun. I brought famous architects together with young people and we conducted worldwide research. We did it all in less than two years. Maybe it was not so special as Venice – I know that – but at the same time I felt that, by doing this research and bringing together all these different people from different countries, we gave it back to the public. I have been in Venice for two or three days now. I have enjoyed it, and I did like the rhythm and sequence that you, Sam, explained earlier. It's almost like a movie: the different rooms in the Arsenale. I did like Bahrain's pavilion, and India's. But I also like the idea that in all these different national pavilions, and all over the city, people are doing their research and creating their laboratories – each in their own way. I want to propose this other way of thinking about biennales.

Conversation Two
New York

Storefront for Art and Architecture, New York:
Paella Series 01

This conversation took place on 7 November 2010. It was organised by Eva Franch i Gilabert, Aaron Levy and William Menking.

Brett Steele: The fundamental reality of contemporary architectural culture is that it is a thing made by a few for a few others, with little broad impact, presence or interest. In a world where niche fields like modern macroeconomics have found a way to communicate to mass audiences – I've just finished reading *SuperFreakonomics* – and the hard sciences have voices in people like Hawking, Dawkins, Gould or others who write books that find their way to every other coffee table in America, the question remains why architecture is so obscure and irrelevant in any other form than magazines like *Dwell* and *Interiors*, or *Architectural Digest*. It's a paradox, given architecture's inherently public presence and face, and even more depressing seeing how the art world has found a way to reinvent itself – post-Warhol, Jeff Koons and Damien Hirst – and have mass presence, appeal and recognition.

This is the point that keeps me focused as the director of a school.

The AA is a school that seeks to invent audiences, not architects. It is the bigger challenge, and the one thing the young careers that we launch need for their futures – compatible and engaged audiences for ideas that today seem alien, strange or incomprehensible. Today's audiences are active agents, not passive entities. Hence the rise of conspiracy theories as the most active and genuinely public form of contemporary theory. Making books whose purpose is to launch unexpected audiences rather than a reader response is one of our aims. Schools and books make audiences, not architects. Audiences rock, and readers – like reader reception theory – are long dead.

Andres Lepik: Look, it all depends on where you present the exhibition. I come here from the Museum of Modern Art in New York, where there's a different audience than you would have for a show at the AA in London. I would say two or three per cent of the MoMA audience is interested in architecture shows. The three million visitors that come to the museum, come for the art. They come for Picasso, Matisse, and then if they see an architecture exhibition, they go in because they're interested in the subject. They don't come for architecture, and they don't go to the architecture exhibition first, because it's not their reason for visiting the institution. So we have to take this into consideration: what is the public expecting when they go to an architecture exhibition? I think it all depends on where you show it.

Prem Krishnamurthy: It's interesting you should say that. Reading *Architecture on Display*, I recall Vittorio Gregotti saying that he wasn't that interested in a broad audience, and that he ultimately felt these things ought to communicate to a specialised audience. The idea of communicating architecture, at least in a mediated form and to a broader public, was seen as a quixotic or a useless endeavour. And that's interesting to me. Today, why does scale automatically signal equality, as opposed to measuring the engagement of that public or its involvement after the fact? Why is quantity automatically expressed as a quality?

Srdjan Jovanovic Weiss: Gregotti also talked about the delayed effects of his exhibition. He wasn't interested in the immediate effect. Of course, he can claim it was a success now, after so many years. So that's my question for tonight: can a delay be used in a strategic way, even to justify a sort of neglect of audiences, when speaking about such a pointed subject as design in architecture?

Ariane Lourie Harrison: If the seeds of an exhibition are linked to students, then this represents a kind of delay as well. It seems that this most recent Venice Biennale is an example of this, for instance with the Architecture Saturdays events, and the university programmes.

William Menking: With regards to this question of delay, I think Gregotti was trying to build an institution, and perhaps an institution represents, more than anything else, the idea of a system whose effects are felt not by its immediate public but by those who come after. I think this idea was linked to the student protests of 1968, which closed down the art biennale at the time with their demands for a more responsive institution. This event, by the way, is the subject of Marco De Michelis' recent piece in *Log*. I think that Gregotti and the other directors of the biennale thought that architecture could span the formalism of art and the political questions posed by the students, and was somehow more reflective of the people.

Eva Franch i Gilabert: Something that I keep hearing lately is that there is too much art in architecture. Just to spur on the conversation: what do you see as art and what do you see as architecture?

Charles Renfro: Isn't one distinction that art is, by definition, always a one-to-one experience? It's never about representation, and that's the choice that we have to make when we exhibit architecture. Kazuyo Sejima did it differently this year: she made almost all of the exhibits one-to-one. They were about the actual experience and actual things, in actual time. Generally speaking, architecture is about showing something that is going to be made or displaying a projection of such a thing. Instead, Sejima argued that with architecture you're actually making an experience and you're making a thing. Those are our choices when we show architecture…

EFG: It's not a space of representation, it's a space of generation …

Aaron Levy: I've been struggling with the idea of what an exhibition can be, as opposed to what it so often is. Does anybody want to make an impassioned defence of the exhibition, despite all the compromises it asks of us? Why do exhibitions still matter today?

WM: To pick up on Aaron's point, maybe the era of the exhibition is over? Maybe it no longer carries the urgency it once did as a means of communication, because of the extreme costs associated with it and the fact that there are now all these other means to communicate architecture digitally?

Mark Wigley: That's a really odd thing for you to say in a gallery. You gather a group of people together in a gallery, with microphones and cameras, for a prospective book and say, 'Could you join with me in announcing the end of exhibitions?' So, basically, you have made an exhibition here, which takes the form of an event at a dinner table. It's an art practice and it's an exhibition practice. Any attempt to rule out exhibitions is unthinkable. As if architecture's gone. And all those curators who say that they are the first people to connect with the public – there are many stupid things you could say as curator of a Venice Biennale, and that is one of the biggest. As if there is something like the public waiting to receive a message from architects. The public is a concept: it is a spatial concept; it's an architectural concept. Even a public that's not listening to you is in your world, and the whole idea that the Venice Biennale would be the place in which you would connect with the public … The level of hypocrisy is astonishing. Venice is a place of retreat from the world; it's a military location. It's very difficult to get to, very expensive to get to, and very difficult to maintain. It's a place of minimum contact with the public.

But I want to get back to my first point about exhibitions. If architecture is unthinkable outside of exhibitions, then that is in itself exhibitionistic from beginning to end. Exhibitions are also weird in that they do not need to be seen. Nor does architecture – the most obvious case being the great buildings of history, where we don't really have much evidence that they were seen. Cedric Price told this absurdly beautiful story about a union called the Harriers who were responsible for picking up dead horses in London. But there was a delay between your horse dying and its being picked up – it would tend to lie in the street for a while. His argument was that it was very difficult to negotiate the steps of the parliament building, say, without fainting – the stench was so overwhelming. So the idea that you would see the architecture and simply luxuriate in its Gothic aspects is misplaced. Even with something like the Parthenon – a building around which a whole city organised its rituals – we really don't have any evidence that it was necessarily seen as such.

Lydia Kallipoliti: I completely agree with this statement, that architecture outside the exhibition format is unthinkable. But I'm just wondering: what is the historical turning point at which the Venice Biennale, and the kind of exhibition that it fostered, was institutionalised to broadcast to an international audience of architects? I am far from an expert on the history of the biennale, but from just leafing through the interviews in the first volume of *Architecture on Display* it seems that the first directors, like Gregotti, didn't exactly know what they were doing when they were setting up their exhibition. It was more a case of putting together things that were in the air at the time, like political activism. And the first shows of the biennale focused on specific topics like the revival of Islamic architecture, and so forth. But then there was a turning point where it became an arena for broadcasting and less concerned with fostering this underground movement than it was with establishing certain figures in the world.

I'm a little suspicious when a curator says 'This is my statement, this is what I'm going to do', because then the exhibition tends to become an instrument to accomplish this agenda, rather than addressing a developing condition. I love Hans Hollein's title *The Architect as Seismograph*, which implies a sort of latency, because we can't predict exactly when an earthquake will occur, we just know that it will happen somewhere, that there are vibrations and waves below the earth and that there's something going on that we can register in a kind of field – but we don't know the location. And I was very interested in that concept.

After 2000, with Massimiliano Fuksas and all the rest that followed, I think the biennale became this institutionalised tool for publicising architects and creating or regimenting a star system. So, I'm just wondering, what was behind this turning point?

Ken Saylor: A lot of people would go back to Paolo Portoghesi and his exhibition, which was produced by Cinecittà and was one of the first large-scale theatrical productions of architecture in the biennale. Within the catalogue you were presented with two-dimensional representations of facades along the corridor of the Arsenale – this became a style-book for many architecture students. It was also important in setting up a larger discursive framework around theories of postmodernism.

But I find the theatrical model somewhat problematic in that, exactly as you described, it attempts to broadcast this kind of spectacle to an unknown public. And if we back up a second and speak more generally of the early biennales, I think that with any exhibition – of architecture or otherwise – there's a kind of social promise, which is that intent, content and communication will be delivered. This can take any number of forms, from the most didactic, which we see in Gregotti, to more pedagogical exhibitions, like Bill's and Aaron's, to the theatrical. The other thing to look at today is the number of practitioners who engage in exhibition design, myself included. There's a wide variety of people, from artists to architects, curators to philosophers, sometimes even set designers. And what one finds are interesting hybrids, each contextually specific, which produce some sort of successful device for communicating to whoever we think our public is. So this idea of the loud blast, of something amplified or broadcast at this very generalised or unspecified scale, doesn't work for me.

PK: Ken, the notion of exhibition that you're using is an expanded notion of exhibition, going beyond what happens for a specific duration within a space that displays one thing or another. I'm just wondering if we want to try to come to a definition of what we're talking about when we say 'exhibition', to figure out what the common understanding is. I heard an interesting talk by Boris Groys earlier today. He was premiering his new book and talking about installation as an idea, and about Facebook as an installation of the self. When I hear something like 'Architecture only happens in exhibition' I want to know when the first exhibitions actually happened in a public sphere. Is there a particular point, historically speaking, perhaps sometime in the eighteenth century?

MW: The site of exhibition has been subjected to radical experimentation for a hundred years or so, and even the most traditional definition of exhibition has super-expanded. The nice way to say it is that I think exhibitions are really weird. But the experience of exhibitions, the powerful utopian impulses that are liberated in them, the amazingly effective and efficient simulations that are constructed … I mean, the whole thing is sort of surreal. And once you embrace that surreal condition of a normal exhibition, then architectural blogs – which could be considered a new form of exhibition – look relatively tame and unprovocative. But I think it would be good to go through the exercise of what doesn't count as an exhibition for everyone here. I, for one, think that tonight is an exhibition. But maybe that's too easy, and we need a better example …

Martin Beck: One way to go would be to distinguish between the terms 'display' and 'exhibition'. Exhibition is more the classical concept of a physical experience in a physical space, where a person walks around and looks at something. And display is a condition of being on view, as well as a method of presenting things to be viewed. In that regard, I've argued a few times that if you see the exhibition as a medium, it is easier to think of it as a medium that is specific to modernity: you could read it from the early exhibitions in the nineteenth century to an almost contemporary Benjaminian condition. Everyone's talking about exhibitions today and maybe there's a reason for that. Maybe that kind of experience of being physically in a space, and looking at a space, is no longer the prevalent form for distributing information.

> Florian Idenburg: But I do think that exhibitions should be about the idea of bringing people together, not just about the individual interacting with the subject they're looking at. There's a communal experience that's being addressed here. I think for Sejima it was really important that people come together in architecture. The blog, the virtual display or the distribution of information, is something very different. In that sense, I would argue that it is not an exhibition.

Nader Vossoughian: If you take MoMA as a case study, I think they're probably more in the business of collecting people than they are in the business of collecting works of art. And that's not a slight against the institution, it's a statement about our times: when we go to museums, in some ways we're looking to experience ourselves, and we can't do that unless we're somehow on display. I think that's something we acutely feel, that if it's not documented then somehow it didn't happen, hence didn't matter.

ALH: But that show requires a distinct time-frame. And I think one of the interesting things about exhibitions is the way they sometimes use a commercial logic: if you create a distinct beginning and an expiration date, people will feel a kind of urgency to attend. Looking at this recent phenomenon of pairing architects and fashion designers in these pop-up shops under the High Line even, architecture has begun to frame a stage for another set of very temporary shows. But I think that bracketing time always remains crucial. Maybe we can add that to the definition of exhibition, that we always need a clear time-frame.

Another question that the biennale presents to me has to do with its successful replication. I believe there are now biennales in nearly every major city around the world. In around 2000 to 2003, we started to see this kind of replication happening everywhere.

Diana Darling: I am not a historian; I am perhaps representative, if anything, of the public. If you are going to an exhibition like a biennale, you have no context forward or backward, and I think it's hard for the public to understand architecture because it's different to just looking at a painting. You have this mixture – especially at the biennale – and it's not really architecture in a classical sense.

NV: What's so complicated? I don't get it.

Michael Young: It goes back to Charles's earlier comment about art and representation, and the meditation on what constitutes a public and who we're making things for. So much of what we do actually can't be put on display for consumption in the typical way that a work of art can be. The representations we make are an expert practice. I remember a few years ago my architecture friends coming up to me and saying 'Hey did you hear about this Zaha Hadid thing that's going on at the Guggenheim?' For better or worse, that exhibition had a much broader public impact than our typical architecture exhibitions. And its success was emblematic of a certain type of spectacle, which I think is one of the issues that is brought up again and again. How do we engage with spectacular representations, objects, models and images? Are there larger issues that they're tied to, that take more time and expertise to get into? Often the public is not there to get into those issues, or it goes over their heads.

Shohei Shigematsu: Shouldn't we talk about the relation between art and architecture exhibitions? For example, how many art exhibitions are happening, compared with architecture exhibitions? If there were as many architecture exhibitions as there were art, then architecture would probably find a communicative form or methodology. But the business model doesn't allow us to do that.

CR: But our exhibition is our built work. I think that's your point – that architecture is its own display mechanism and the success of our practices often depends on it actually being realised. It doesn't need to be in galleries: rather than making representations of a future thing, why aren't we making the experience itself? I think that's sort of the issue.

KS: I think there are interesting historical examples that actually achieve both. If you look at the history of modernity and the propagandistic nature of the demonstration house …

MB: I think architecture is at a big disadvantage, because in an art exhibition what you are looking at is actually happening right there, in front of you. And if you look at an architecture exhibition it's always referring to somewhere else as well …

PK: Can I jump in and disagree with this notion that art exhibitions are about one-to-one representation? Since the conceptual practices of the 60s or 70s at least, an art exhibition traces a larger practice than is on display.

It's not just a product or thing: you're buying into the process of that artist. So this distinction that the art exhibition entails a sort of presence – well, it's total nonsense.

I'm shocked to hear people talking about how art or architecture actually functions in this or that way, when in both cases it's the representation of a process that is on display. You're talking about something that is the trace of something that is always larger.

CR: You're intellectualising it. Art – unless it's something like an earthwork, like *Spiral Jetty*, is not a projection about something that is to be. It is there on the spot at that moment.

PK: Well it's both things, and it's the same thing in architecture exhibitions. You have the presence of the things that are there as themselves …

Andre Singer: But there's also an inverse relationship at play here. Buildings are by definition in contact with the public at large, but when the practice of architecture is shown, self-consciously or with intent, in an exhibition, it reaches a much smaller audience. A lot of you are curators, and I'm actually a developer. If we were to have a lot of architects here we'd have a completely different debate. Their problem, in a way, is that they reach such a wide public, and that in itself creates difficulties or stresses – and also of course opportunities.

MW: I like what you're saying, and it fits very well with Michael's point about the business model. Because in terms of the big discussion – what counts as an exhibition? – I'd stretch this definition further than other people might want to. I would want to say that in every historical moment a very different concept of exhibition is operational. I want to honour the specificity of techniques and so on, but I also want to challenge everybody to run the thing backwards. For example, do we consider a Gothic cathedral to be an exhibition piece? It's not so easy, this argument about whether it is or not. The building's immobility made it inaccessible to the art market that was soon to come in France – with the removal of paintings and sculptures from the Gothic cathedrals to the Louvre. In other words, the potential mobility of the art object, which allows it to be the engine of a market, creates this opposition with the apparent immobility of the building. There are many other paradoxes too, one of which you have already pointed out: the architect has the problem of having to communicate with too many people, and is therefore not in a good relationship with the few rich people who would be the key, while the reverse is true for the artist. I love the idea of equal opportunities: as long as architects feel burdened by immobility, their objects cannot move, and therefore cannot be bought and sold and cannot participate in the market.

I want to go back to Brett's comment, because it may also have within it the idea of the business model. The question of what is an exhibition and what is not is actually one of training. It goes back to who is being trained to experience a Gothic cathedral in a particular way. It absolutely fits the idea of a choreographed experience, it fits the idea of an experience loaded with particular values, and it also fits the idea of absolute representation. We visit a Gothic cathedral in order to leave our world behind and go to another world, so it's an object that creates a bridge between the two worlds. It is the über-representation, more than any art object can be today. But I think Brett's comments don't go quite far enough. The many curators of the Venice Biennale act as if there is a public waiting to be communicated with, but this concept of the public is an artwork – it is such a manufactured product, such a fragile and ephemeral thing. Architecture, the art that is known for its immobility – the fact that it doesn't move and that it's stuck there, stuck in a sort of fixed relationship that it cannot defeat on any level – economic, personal, physical or emotional – is the art that really dreams of a redefinition of experience.

So in a way, the problem with architects is that they're just way too ambitious. If the architect's ambition were simply to sell a product, we would be with the artists in a second. Some of my best friends are artists, and they're always astonished at the business naivety of architects. Many of today's most successful architects have taken their entire practice from art. They make houses, they make spaces, with one difference: they subtract the ambition to renew the entire nature of experience, and just say no, we are going to sell a particular experience to a particular audience that we have carefully constructed. So in a way, the problem with architects (though there are many problems) is that they're really romantic in a way that artists have no time for. It's a waste of time, this romance.

EFG: Architecture should be able to create a desire for those things that still do not exist in any other medium, and I think that's an area where architects sometimes fail. Rather than 'display', I am interested in the moment when representation becomes a space of generation, the moment when an exhibition becomes a space of departure in itself. When we look at the public we usually see people who are going to consume ideas, projects, products. The moment you give the public a desire to create, to participate, you change the entire game. And so for me, the concept of 'display' lacks desire, lacks nerve and tension. The idea of display, and of the exhibition, is quite dead, or it should be quite dead. And for that reason I think that Sejima's biennale was great. Her intent was to move away from that logic of representation towards a logic of sensation, which was extremely powerful for me.

ALH: It's interesting that in this discussion of display we seem to be talking about singular objects or experiences, whereas I thought there was an understanding that an exhibition is a framework in which a series of carefully selected items or things are asked to dialogue with each other. And that is where the public can enter. It's not just about the relationship between things, it is also about trying to investigate and position the public as a reader between objects.

MW: The immobility of architecture is not a given: it's a cultural fantasy. Whatever role that architects have in society – and it's minimal – is given to us because we have access to that fantasy – those images of security, stability and so on. Immobility actually gives architects exciting opportunities. I think artists are burdened by the apparent demand to be original, subversive and creative – it's just such an impossible burden. So there is a difference between what architects are told, right from the beginning –

that they can never be interesting, and if they're interesting then they're no longer architects – and what we say to artists – that they are destined to be forever interesting – and architects have somehow to solve that paradox so that they can brand themselves as always interesting in the same way. Between those two things, there is room for a lot of experimentation.

NV: I think we're using caricatured ideas about artists and architects. I teach architectural history, and the history of architecture over the last 150 years is virtually interchangeable with the history of architectural exhibitions. Whether you're talking about the 1852 Crystal Palace Exhibition, the L'Esprit Nouveau pavilion of 1925, MoMA and the international style exhibition, Weissenhof, well, it goes on and on. The notion that architecture is immobile is itself a fantasy – at least inasmuch as you judge the history of architecture by the canon as we define it. Certainly art is not just about immediacy, either, unless you understand the context around it. Since Duchamp in particular, the history of art is inextricably connected to the discourse that surrounds it. So to say that art is somehow immediate and architecture is somehow mediated I think is a gross misconception that ignores 150 years of history.

MB: I think I have to rehabilitate my earlier comment, because I was cut off before I could finish. What I was trying to get at, if I can keep using Mark's example of the Gothic cathedral, was this distinction between one kind of exhibition where you're actually here, and the other kind, in which that Gothic cathedral and the experience are represented in another space. Those are two different kinds of things, and there is a tension there that comes out between art and architecture. And of course there's always a reference to something else within art as well, no doubt about that.

MW: You're right, yet when we go back to the Gothic cathedral, we don't simply cross a line between the object and the representation of the object.

MB: No, it's a fluid border, but there are two typologies, as Ken used the term.

MW: It's surely different, but the difference doesn't take us outside the discussion of exhibition: it's another moment in the history of exhibition. You might say that exhibition history proper begins when you take a photograph of that Gothic cathedral and then bring it into another space, or country, or city. I'm inclined to say, though, that even the infrastructure of the Gothic cathedral was exactly that kind of displacement, that bringing of images of another place.

PK: And of course there's that in-between state, a space of pedagogy – a Gothic cathedral is a space for the transmission of ideas. I thought your point before about duration was interesting, and of course relates to this question of immobility. It makes you think: is the idea of a permanent installation a contradiction in itself?

MB: Well, we had these architecture exhibitions in Berlin in the 1950s and the 80s, and some are still standing, still exhibitions.

PK: Exactly. Is it conceivable that an exhibition can exist forever? Does duration have to be part of the idea of an exhibition as we understand it?

ALH: I always feel that duration is fundamental to the commercial logic. It's always the planned obsolescence that guarantees a certain audience's participation. I'm perhaps being a little cynical here, but I am asking to what degree the public would be motivated without an expiration date, at which point the exhibition vanishes? And this is where a blog comes in, as it allows you to revisit and follow the record of the conversations. For me, paradoxically, the blog has a stability, while the exhibition in its definitive time-frame insists that you make that movement. And perhaps that's where the exhibition has a little more to do with ancient paradigms

71

of pilgrimage, definitive time movements and the rhythms of time. We could ask if even the Venice Biennale benefits from the kind of regular interval that structures a life.

CR: Isn't what you're illustrating the difference in expertise? The blog is, by definition, not going to be the voice of an expert. Yet an exhibition is typically moderated, curated and put together by an expert – not always, but generally. And so there's really a major difference between stuff that's supposed to go online, that's open source if you will, versus this table which is curated as a group of experts, and privileges expertise.

PK: Why should we trust an exhibition, rather than a blog? We haven't addressed the question of ideology within exhibitions – propaganda exhibitions were one of the best examples of architectural display throughout the twentieth century. Exhibitions are precisely what we shouldn't trust, because they are so seductive. We go into a room that we can only walk through in a certain way, and there's a certain lighting scheme, and it might smell a certain way. Whereas when we read something on a blog, we do that in our own home, in the conditions that we have chosen, and we can determine how our body is situated. We just can't do those things in an exhibition.

KS: Well you're talking about two radically different modes of social reception. New media promises us many things, but we're as separate as we are together when we engage in social media. If I can pull this back to notions around reception: ideally within the space of an exhibition I'm trying to get at an active participant, an active audience that collaborates in the production of meaning. But the social and discursive space within a physical exhibition is really very different from that of a blog.

MY: What do we see as the most instrumental in terms of spurring on or changing the discourse that we all deal with? Is it exhibitions, publications, competitions? Honestly, it's not the Venice Biennale that has spurred on the shifts and changes within the last 20 years of architectural thought.

EFG: What was it, then?

MY: Competitions, actually. As an architect and as a designer, competitions are crucial to changing the way I think about things.

EFG: So do you see competitions as a way of curating as well?

MY: Potentially. You have to think about how those competitions are displayed, how they're disseminated and how they're given out to the public at large.

MW: This is sort of irrelevant, but I refuse to go to biennales because I consider them to be the height of kitsch. It's like being at a supermarket for our field. It seems to me that to look to the biennale for evidence of new direction in our field is the equivalent of looking to the Oscars to find out where movies are going. I don't think any of us would do that. We should look at Venice the other way around, and say that its role is actually to create a sense of hierarchy, of who's approved and who's not. It is not a representation of where the field is going, but of what the field will allow to be said of itself in an official setting. What's interesting about Venice is the extent to which its inability to control its own dimensions allows for certain things to occur that are genuinely productive. I'm always taken by Beatriz [Colomina]'s argument that Mies's Barcelona pavilion, which was arguably the most influential exhibition project ever, was not seen by anybody in the field, and was not seen by the experts. To not be seen and to be overlooked is the key.

NV: This is the kind of difficult discussion that ends up with a clichéd question like 'which pavilion did you like the most?' – which then almost has to be your statement. On that note,

could those of you who attended say which
pavilion you liked?

EFG: I think it is important to talk about the
biennale not just in terms of the most successful
projects, but also according to the lowest
denominator. Is censorship actually possible?

PK: It is interesting to think about the things
within the pavilions, and why they were made
the way they were. And did they succeed or fail?
And if they failed badly, then why – was it on
account of the people involved, or a systematic
problem? Transposing to my own field, when
I think about the exhibiting of graphic design,
I always wonder why it is presented as an auton-
omous practice or object that exists in the
world without any sort of context or explanation, when in fact it ought to be exhibited in
such a way that you understand the decisions
and the people who made it possible. And I
wonder the same thing about architecture. By
looking at each biennale in that way, you are
asking how it also functions within the representation of architecture.

ALH: But perhaps in evaluating failure, we should
remember how important failures are – going back
to the Weissenhof exhibition and its critique as
kitschy. The kitsch quality that Mark has referred

to is important, because, going in, you understand the kitsch and have accepted that. Perhaps the public is a lot more attuned to the kitsch, and savours it as much as anyone else who understands that framework.

SJW: I was not at the Venice Biennale, but I do have a favourite pavilion. It is a failed pavilion: the pavilion of Croatia, which was built on a raft and sent over the sea. It collapsed and was sent back – so nobody has seen it and it wasn't judged. And I think it is actually my favourite pavilion, just because it was not there.

NV: The perfect show is the one we all never saw.

MW: This is a question then: does this eminent dinner party have an example of an exhibition whose viewers felt that their whole world had changed after seeing it? Of the few exhibitions that are reputed to be game-changers, there is no evidence of audience reaction – and that includes *This is Tomorrow*, in 1956, about which I know quite a lot. This doesn't mean that the exhibition was anonymous, but there is no evidence that the art community, whatever that might mean, had any reaction to that show. And yet, there is no history of twentieth-century art that does not refer to that exhibition. One could almost imagine a kind of a hypothetical alternative theory, which is to say that by definition any show that has the capacity to change the perception of a field is invisible to that field – its influence is perceivable only retroactively. Exhibitions always carry the potential to be appropriated as game-changers. Then the role of the curator would be to, as it were, spin the wheel and just set up something that is sufficiently well documented to make it a candidate for revisionist histories – and if you are smart, you participate in those revisionist histories. Don't forget, for example, that two of the critics involved in the *This is Tomorrow* exhibition – Reyner Banham, indirectly, and Lawrence Alloway, directly – were probably, at that moment, the most influential critics in their respective fields. Alloway went directly to MoMA and Banham was probably the most eloquent spokesperson for architecture at that time. So the trick would be to make yourself an exhibition that nobody understands, so it's overlooked, but make sure you have in place a certain number of models and key people, and if those people turn out to be successes in their careers, you might get dragged along with them. And that's the best you can do.

Levy: In our conversation with Portoghesi, we came to understand that his brilliance was not to be found in the actual exhibition itself, but rather in the infrastructure that he left behind for future exhibitions. In renovating the Corderie, he made possible not only future exhibitions but the institution's future as well. That is, in my mind, a good example of an overlooked but remarkably strategic gesture. His was an exhibition that, fundamentally, makes it possible for others to exhibit after.

KS: But it also radically transformed Venice …

NV: They talk a lot about the Venice Biennale and its impact on the city at this point. How has Venice changed in the interim, in the last 30 years?

KS: Simultaneously there's a kind of corporate patronage being inflicted on Venice, so that in a way the city is for sale as well. As Aaron and Bill have pointed out before, there are so many corporate interventions in Venice that are affecting the museum city, not dissimilar to what we find if we look at other museums and their contemporary corporatisation, their branding exercises, sponsorships and donors.

Chiara Barbieri: As a Venetian, I think of the relationship between the biennale and the city of Venice as one of conflict. The city of Venice does not perceive the biennale as part of it. What the biennale gives to the city is minor –

aside from the hoteliers, who are very happy. There is really no interaction, and although the city of Venice always wants to have more interaction with the institution, the institution is somewhat closed. So the city of Venice, in a way, feels deprived of the Giardini and the national pavilions. The biennale takes over this public park for about six months of the year, and keeps fighting with the city over its maintenance. But the biennale has recently done something amazing: it has convinced the Ministry of Defence, which owns the Arsenale (because it's still part of the naval base), to hand over the part that the biennale has restored. Yet the Arsenale as a whole remains closed, and the only piece that the city can use is the tiny theatre in which the biennale gives its general press conference. The city of Venice is small – I am one of 60,000 residents who are 'invaded' by 1.2 million tourists a year. My life there is difficult from this point of view. So if you want to look at Venice from the architectural point of view, what Venice needs is housing.

Levy: As the manager of the US pavilion you have a unique vantage-point on contemporary architecture and its curation. Every year you watch the biennale be produced, in all its messiness, and you yourself also have a role in its production. Every year you oversee an elaborate choreography behind the scenes that never gets disclosed to the public because it's not part of the display.

> CB: Sure, but at the same time this Byzantine process is what happens in every single museum, or in every single location in which an exhibition is organised. It is not necessarily the process that should be on stage, because it is part of all of our jobs to arrive at that point.

BS: I want to steer the conversation in a different direction for a moment. To me, books are the most interesting kind of performance today because they require the participation of culture's most threatened species: the editor. As Gordon Lish has argued, editing is where all the real writing gets done today. The contemporary battle between curators and editors is requiring us all to pick sides. Everything is called curating today. I am naturally suspicious and will always pick the underdog in any good fight, and so in the world of architectural production I go with editors over curators any day of the week. Let's recall that modern architecture was invented in the early years of the twentieth century, simultaneous with the rise of modern publishing industries. Gropius, Corb, even Mies, were all distinguished editors before they were builders. Even Wright reinvented himself middle-aged with his own entire re-editing of his career, in the Wasmuth portfolio. Editors invented what we now call modern architecture; my hunch is that they can invent for us a way out of it.

PK: It's the thing that lasts the longest, other than the building. The exhibition is over, and the catalogue is what ultimately makes careers, and makes things be remembered.

ALH: Publishing has traditionally been a place in which contemplation was possible because it takes time to make a book. But I think one of the shifts that links back to the discussion of the blog is the ability to publish online at speed – it's wild how fast we can actually publish today. Perhaps this raises the question: is there a certain trade-off between response and reflection? Is that useful? Where do we stand regarding the fact that a book is going to be the only stable element of an exhibition?

PK: I'm sure that anybody here who makes exhibitions can attest to the fact that they usually only come together in the last two days. You are installing right up to the last moment. What exhibition is ever done when it should be done? And the catalogue comes out simultaneously with the exhibition, probably completed under extreme duress. That kind of publishing is a different thing from the other kind of publishing we are talking about. These records of exhibitions are themselves very specific documents that happen super-fast. And maybe this makes them more revealing documents than a monograph that takes five years to put together.

MB: That's also one of the interesting things though – the relationship between publications and exhibitions, because most of these publications do not represent the exhibition at all. So as viewers we have to project how these exhibitions functioned, and are thus the prime victims of mythology. People keep talking about Portoghesi's *Strada Novissima*. Even when people say they haven't actually seen it they still insist it's the most important thing the biennale has ever done. And that sort of discrepancy is fascinating, between the catalogue that has to be ready on the day the show opens and the show being finished ten minutes later, and the reality that there's still no record of it.

LK: I would argue that what you were saying about the expediency of the catalogue – the fact that it has to be out on the day the exhibition opens – is really an advantage in getting 'raw material' into print. It takes out all the filters that are generally in use.

CR: We are showing our lack of faith in the digital world here by talking about books, because isn't the archive ultimately going to be digital? Who really cares about books?

NV: Paradoxically, events can garner attention in the public imagination in the way that digital media and books can't. People don't read books. I think that the exhibition is really the most vital way in which people in our respective fields can engage a broad audience today – period. That has been my experience.

MW: But you have a nostalgia there, right? I remember when I was about to publish my first book and I said to this friend of mine, Larry Rickels, that I had to get used to the idea of people reading it. He said no, you have to get used to the idea that people don't read books. I found that incredibly liberating. And I would say that with books it's the same as with exhibitions. The purpose of an exhibition is not to be seen, but to have a good party that will allow the people who are engaged to engage with each other. It's the same with books. The purpose of books is not to be read. I buy books not to read them. I own a lot of books. I write books, I collect books, I think about books, I copy books, I pay for books – I'm in the book business. But I don't read books. Don't assume that exhibitions are meant to be seen, and that books are meant to be read. Buildings are by and large invisible, and that's to their credit.

83

AS: Words are not meant to be heard! I don't agree with this at all. So why are you talking?

MW: Well, according to my theory you don't need to ask me! Look, I am wary of isolating exhibitions and books and famous buildings. But over time there will be exhibitions that will retroactively be reconstructed as highly symbolic. The action of constructing them is highly symbolic. It will involve huge violence to what occurred. It will generally be easier to do if there is no evidence of what happened. The same with books: *Delirious New York*, *Complexity and Contradiction*, *Toward an Architecture*, *Learning from Las Vegas* – are we really saying that these books, which are among the five or six most influential books in the last 100 years, have been genuinely *read* by architects? No, they just act as kinds of totems of a certain direction of thinking. I like the idea that we just, for example, increase the number of exhibitions and the opportunities for more creative history writing, and then more creative things will happen. Can you think of any exhibition in which people from a field went to that exhibition, and their life changed and their field changed?

AS: I would make the opposite argument. The way you're talking: you're looking at learning and how, when you learn, you don't really change. But there is a difference between learning and experiencing. And when you experience things, you do change. I would say that what you are defining is learning, and to that extent I agree with you. Where I absolutely do not agree with you is on the value of experience: it can take the form of an exhibition or a building – it can be anything.

MW: Yes, I can see the difference between learning and experience. But experience also includes not going. In other words, I can choose not to go to the Venice Biennale, and yet, given what people have told me about it, that can be as positive an experience as somebody who went, based on the very same description.

LK: So let's ask of you, in summary, if you are talking about an afterlife. Are you talking about how there is a phantom being produced after the event, and the phantom produces a new reality, which is the reality that reconstitutes the subject itself?

MW: I don't believe in experience, basically. To get back to the *This is Tomorrow* exhibition: I have some knowledge about this exhibition, more than most. But that kind of understanding in no way offers me any special opportunity to understand the meaning of that exhibition or the reason this exhibition had the effect that it did. What I can tell you is that it has nothing to do with what was on display in those rooms, and what was experienced by the people who saw it. Nevertheless, this is without doubt an absolutely pivotal exhibition. In other words, exhibitions could not be more important, but the actual experience of an actual exhibition has no relation to their importance. That would be my opinion, and it comes in the form of this very silly claim: tell me an exhibition that has, in its almost phenomenological reality, changed people's minds.

PK: I don't think it's facile to ask whom an exhibition actually changes. It may not change the people who see the thing, it may be irrelevant whether they see it, read a review or see pictures of it later. It may be important that it changes the people who were involved in it. That would be an interesting lineage.

SJW: It would be great to brainstorm about which exhibitions should have been done, or could be recovered. I think that would be a great way at least to think about exhibitions, which is not the past as past, but the past as a future.

MW: It seems to me that it is possible to say nothing is more important than exhibitions. But it doesn't follow that what's important is the experience of exhibitions. The exhibition is just an extraordinary opportunity to elaborate a mythology, and it's multimedia by nature. It involves so many dimensions that we've already talked about. It's not just the exhibition versus the book. Every exhibition has a book, but it also has design, graphic design and architecture. Maybe our current concept of exhibition is somewhat narrow and there will be a wider one in the future. To make an exhibition is to try to place a mythology across the full bandwidth of our field. Now, success doesn't mean that everybody listens. Actually, if everybody listens it means there's a problem, it means you're not saying anything. Success is probably very un-clear, and it is for sure a retroactive phenome-non. Exhibitions are where the stakes are high-er. Everybody here talks about the fact that they last for a short time, but exhibitions are forever. They're monumental! But buildings come and go, buildings only last 20, 30, 100 years.

Beatriz Colomina: You cannot think about modern architecture without thinking about all these tem-porary sites of exhibitions. Exhibitions are forms of architecture, and sites of innovation in architecture. The fact that the times for preparing an exhibition are shorter is actually more conducive to experi-mentation, which you cannot do in a building site. Most of the breakthroughs in architecture have not happened in the buildings, but in the exhibit. You can look at the history of architecture, and the most interesting moments turn out to be ephemeral. The concept of the exhibition that I am talking about is not the retrospective, but rather the exhibition as a site of architectural experimentation. Those are the ones I think are worth talking about, and that we remember in time. Look at the case of Mies: his breakthrough didn't happen in the context of a regular client or project. It was only in the context of the Weissenhof, which is an exhibition after all, and the context of the Barcelona pavilion, that he was able to break through.

> PK: What you're saying is that memory, even in a kind of transformed way, exists indefinitely. The building itself ends but the exhibition exists forever. That is the kind of rhetorical move you are making, and so of course the argument is that the exhibition generates more discussion than the building. The building, as something that exists in a place, is taken for granted because it doesn't have duration, because it seems to exist permanently.

BC: But it's not only that. There is something interesting about exhibitions, and the way that you don't have to deal with a lot of the things that you have to deal with in architecture. So you liberate architectural thinking, and that is what I think is worth claiming.

NV: I agree with that. I think that the exhibition is to architecture what the manifesto is to literature. It allows you to illustrate stuff with a certain diagrammatic clarity.

MB: I would say, more, that the exhibition is the discursive ghost to architecture. We can hardly think of any architecture book of the 1910s or 20s that had the same impact as the exhibitions of the period. These exhibitions – nobody has seen them; they were described in some reviews only peripherally. But what they offer us is a clean slate, onto which we project the facts we know through archival research and the facts we think were there in terms of experience, in terms of just being there – that's what makes them valuable.

MW: I am also tempted to say that it's the ghost from the beginning. Almost by definition, the idea of the exhibition is to construct a ghost – to give shape to something that isn't there. It's just this experimental thing. The role of the show is a mirage, and then it becomes a double mirage because the evidence of the mirage usually disappears.

ALH: But the mirage is often constructed by corporations. If we think about the Werkbund's role ... the Weissenhof needed a very clear system like the biennale which was reliable, which came year after year. We can't disassociate the Weissenhof from corporate funding and the 1930s show of glass manufacturers that followed. I feel we are talking about exhibitions as these powerful registers that are disassociated from the material and financial reality.

> MW: No, ghosts are part of the economy. If ghosts do not play an important functional role in our economy, architects are gone. We say architecture is not just building, but building architecture is the part we offer. Weissenhof was a ghost, a mirage. It was not a representation of an existing movement of contemporary architects, it was not a representation even of its own rules! Mies insisted that an off-white should be used, and then he used pink. Architects, we make mirages in stone. We make ghosts tangible. We are in the business of making this kind of palpable sensation. And I love this idea that the sort of ultimate trajectory of an exhibition is in the area of the ghost.

EFG: For the ghost to exist, it has to defy notions of reality. Architecture and exhibitions, as ghosts, are able to defy materiality, economy, politics – anything that consists of what I would consider the real matter of everyday life. That is what I think architecture exhibitions should do.

MW: 1932, the MoMA exhibition: Philip Johnson and Alfred Barr make an image of modern architecture, but not a false one. It was in fact a particular, productive fantasy that they believed. They believed that a certain image of European modern architecture – a certain image, it's not for us to say true or false – is the inevitable future of this discipline. And they package it and make it available to a mass market. They construct ghosts, but the ghosts are real. The 1932 show is as influential as Weissenhof – perhaps more so. And why is it influential? Because of the incredible level of fantasy involved. And they are very particular about it. So what's brilliant is that this is from a man who had not even trained as an architect yet. Johnson makes the most influential architecture exhibition in the twentieth century and says: 'I could become an architect.' Johnson and Barr construct a mirage, self-consciously and with enormous professionalism. This mirage becomes useful, even for the architects whose work is mistreated in this way. No greater fantasy could Le Corbusier and his buddies have had than to establish a normative set of aesthetic principles.

Conversation Three London

Architectural Association School, London

This conversation took place on 7 March 2011. It was organised by Roberta Jenkins, Aaron Levy, William Menking and Brett Steele.

Brett Steele: A book is not an empty document but a way of opening up conversations and discussions that wouldn't otherwise take place. I'm super keen on that as a project – in part because for many decades architecture, like other forms of culture, has eroded into increasingly monologue forms of thinking. Things such as the evening lecture series here at the AA School are modelled on the idea that I can just stand up and tell you about the way architecture is – present my version of the universe. This is very different to the kind of model that has shaped modern architecture as we know it, where people have come together and had a discussion or a conversation. By thinking together, we may produce forms of knowledge that any one of us, on our own, could not realise. I'm hoping this conversation can be productive, and that it can in some way start to battle the decline of that particularly European model of thinking that depends upon groups of smart people getting together in rooms and having a conversation, usually over a decent meal and with the hope that the world could get better because of it. I think it's still something we should try to hold on to…

Sean Griffiths: Audiences are a fairly significant part of conversations, but they aren't often mentioned. I suppose one of the interesting things about architectural exhibitions is that they don't display architecture – they display representations of architecture. That creates its own problematic, in that there's immediately a whole series of other questions to consider about how you can represent architecture. I'm interested in an idea that Walter Benjamin raises in 'The Work of Art in the Age of Mechanical Reproduction', which contrasts the way that the tourist looks at architecture – with the rapt attention of the viewer who has specifically gone to look at a piece of architecture as displayed in a real city – with the normative everyday experience of architecture, or haptic experience, as he describes it – which is habitual and disinterested. In a sense, that tension comes closest to the way in which architectural exhibitions work, to the extent that people often go to see architectural exhibitions as an art experience – a mainly visual experience. Exhibitions are a really important part of architectural discourse, in the sense that they are one way in which ideas about architecture might be conveyed to the public who may otherwise be ignorant of them, if they're not involved in occasions like tonight. It would be interesting to have people who are not insiders in a discussion like this. New immersive technologies now allow for a very different experience of architecture – something that might actually replicate the haptic to a certain degree, although it's difficult to see how you would do that with an exhibition, because of the attitude of mind that you bring to it as a viewer.

Shumon Basar: I have spent a number of years intensely engaged with curating exhibitions and thinking about this term that seems to have appeared from nowhere – first, the term curator, and then the neologism curation, which etymologically really has its basis in theology, and which is still not employed by German or French institutions. I think there was something that happened in the 1990s and then in the early 2000s, when it took on a momentum and became a kind of interesting thing. Like many interesting things, it was overexposed and over debated, and I find most of it deeply uninteresting now. In terms of 1968 and the first architectural exhibition at the Venice Biennale, perhaps the engagement that certain architects or architectural students were having with politics and everyday life was in advance of where the art world was at that point. Generally speaking, architecture tends to be behind the art world discursively, and when it comes to questions concerning exhibition and curation, I think it's centuries behind, to the extent that it ends up fantasising crises that I don't think are genuinely that important and the art world has dealt with a long time ago.

I don't know if tautology is the right word, but it's the only one I can use at the moment to make a statement about architecture and exhibitions. Would you ask the same thing about the use of a book today, or the use of a magazine, or the use of a TV show? I read a lecture given by Adrian Forty about one of the things we did at the Design Museum, and he rightfully said that the exhibition is a medium in its own right – it's not a supplement. It's what you get when you add a number of things on a wall in a room and open a bottle of wine. The exhibition has an autonomy and an ontological quality that isn't necessarily superior or inferior to other things. We need to look again at the art world, for instance at books such as Mary Anne Staniszewski's *The Power of Display*, Bruce Altshuler's *The Avant-Garde in Exhibition* or Lewis Kachur's *Displaying the Marvelous*. Art history can still teach us, in looking at the twentieth century, that the canonisation of art, artists and great works has often disregarded the fact that most art comes into the world in the context of the exhibition. It's then codified and retrospectively curated as though

it exists in a kind of vacuum. It's often the case –
particularly with certain kinds of postwar architecture, where there's a divergence between the prag-
matic aspects of the profession and the academic
direction. I sometimes do get a little irate because
I would just ask for greater specificity. Not to you
necessarily, but generally, because otherwise it's this
weird circumnavigation between a set of constantly
generic anxieties that are only genuine in the sense
that they're brought into being by giving them a
name and saying that they exist.

Mark Cousins: Taking up Shumon's point, the
first thing is that once something starts appear-
ing as a topic for MAs, like training in curation,
then it's a dead issue, it's already finished. In
a sense I overlap with Shumon, but I want to
put it in quite a polemical way, because then
there's at least something very provocative on
the table. It's strange that the standards of curation have fallen, while the rise of curatorship as
an issue has massively increased. In my mind,
certainly in England, the great postwar curator
of twentieth-century modernist art was David
Sylvester. I recall that, about 20-odd years ago,
there were two large blockbuster shows about
Francis Bacon. He put one on at the Hayward
Gallery, in London, and he had thought about
that building so long, and about a brilliant but
small selection of works by Bacon. He made the

revolutionary but small gesture of hanging them very low. That move from where they would normally be in an exhibition space to the lower space was full of incalculable consequences, but to many people it would seem that's a small gesture that is hardly worth talking about. This can be contrasted, not that long ago, with the incompetence of the Donald Judd exhibition at Tate Britain, in London, which was curated by Nicholas Serota. It was one of the worst curated shows I've ever seen. In front of Judd, and you could hear the poor man suffering in his grave, they had cheap wooden beading on the floor. I asked what it was for, and they said, 'It's to show people where they mustn't walk.' Anyone who knows Judd knows, through his writings, that his work is based on the relationship between objects and space, and their effects, which means that it would be unthinkable to put that beading down. It was deeply stupid and offensive.

The question I think we have to look at first of all is this rise of curation when it's accompanied with what appears to be a decline in the standards of doing it. The second, slightly provocative, remark I would make is that curation really is the name for what you might call the fifth column, concerning the way in which art is being bureaucratised. That is to say, whatever the imperfections of the previous situation, curation and the rise of the curator as a figure who's mediating between institutions, art objects, raising money, whatever, represents a bureaucratisation of art that can be understood in a number of different ways. First of all, it's the back door through which a kind of censorship is re-emerging. Under the old dispensation, the question for a gallery was whether or not the work they were showing actually was thought to transgress a law. If it was really bad, they sent in the police. I can remember it happening time and time again. Today, it's the funding body that responds by taking away the funding from the gallery. There have been a number of instances in the UK where curators have been advised that the artwork be removed on these grounds. It is not that you are going to be prosecuted; rather, that it will do damage to your public reputation. At a larger level, it represents a hideous discourse of humanism, with the expectation that not only exhibitions but galleries serve a welfare function. That is to say, they've got to be friendly to children, families, and the rest of it. I gave the opening speech when Tony Fretton's Camden Arts Centre, in London, reopened. And I thought that if I'm going to do it, I might as well be provocative. So I said that the remake was good, but I did wish they'd keep one day of the week when you couldn't have children in. As you can imagine, there was suddenly a huge intake of breath in the room, and I was on a knife-edge thinking this could all go very wrong. At which point, thank God, two old ladies in their eighties started clapping.

Under the humanism of curatorship, under this terrible blanket of virtue, exhibitions are made horrible. I'm saying the curator is the instrument of bureaucratisation – biennales are being bureaucratised, a whole lot is being bureaucratised, and you can't divorce it from the rise of the curator. It hurts an old socialist to say this, but public money seems more tainted these days than private money. Private money is just sort of wicked and capricious. Public money is really tainted, and comes with so many different conditions attached. You've got to be virtuous, and polemically I want to oppose the idea.

At the same time, what you might call the problem of arrangement has become much deeper and wider, and you can mark it by that use of the suffix that became widespread about ten years ago – we've got landscapes, we've got datascapes, we've got all sort of -scapes. This obviously has Deleuzian aspects, and arranging things is incredibly important, but it has nothing to do with curation. One last thing concerning Benjamin: in the new translation, the title is 'Art in the Age of Technological Reproducibility', according to the translators and Harvard University Press. It doesn't sound like much of an improvement. Benjamin looks at what he calls a distinction in artwork between cult value and exhibition value. When he says exhibition value, he means it has got to be presented as an object, it's no longer cultic and being used for magical or religious purposes, or something like that. In that sense, we ought to look at the problem of exhibition not as part of the domain of curation, but as how art moves from not being experienced – or what I would call the inhibition of art – to the exhibition of art. It's about the appearance of art, and that's the difficult issue of arrangement. We should not confuse that with curation.

Olympia Kazi: I come from a very different perspective, and maybe it has to do with the fact that I'm not a native English-speaker. So for me, curating within the architecture world is not associated only with exhibitions, as is the case with the arts. There is a mistaken presumption of contrasting architectural curatorship and art curatorship, and that's the wrong paradigm. Architecture is different to art. The architectural world has many different conditions, and when I'm curating architecture, I'm actually interested in orchestrating competitions. For example, a major environmental agency in the US – the Environmental Defense Fund – has been working for 30 years in the lower Mississippi river. After all that time – and after a hundred years of damage being done to that region – they realised there was a need for a new vision. I'm the director of the Van Alen Institute in New York, where we undertake projects in public architecture. Essentially, the lawyers came to the architects, and they asked, 'Could you help us with this?' It was shocking, because usually architects are kept out of the decision-making process and places. I've been working with them now for over a year and a half, and I have a very different perspective on what the role of the architecture curator can be today. There are great things happening in the academy and small grassroots galleries. But how do you bridge this with the discourse of the decision-makers?

Vanessa Norwood: I think there's a problem with the term of curator – it's been almost entirely devalued by being so fashionable. About ten years ago, you could get these badges that said 'Everyone's a DJ'. It said everyone's a fucking DJ because it was true, in that everyone you knew had a couple of decks in their bedroom at home and they all thought they were DJs. And I'd like to say it's the same now with curators. I feel that it's a word that's lost any potency because everybody's doing it, and maybe we need to find another word, a more appropriate word.

John Palmesino: How does this idea of the elite that you're introducing then match with what Mark says? It's either a bureaucracy, or it's an elite. And you cannot have the two unless you think that the entire bureaucratic machinery is somehow concomitant. What we are discussing here is on many levels related to what architecture does constantly: it puts into the world ways of seeing the world itself. In that sense, the notion of display in architecture is redundant. In order to somehow attack this point I think it would be interesting to introduce notions like objectivity into architecture. How do you relate architectural discourse and practice to the rise of the discourse of objectivity and the rationality of objectivity? How does the world come into vision through complex processes of subjectification, production and labour?

William Menking: Would you object to the idea set forth by many past directors of the Venice Biennale of Architecture that architecture can somehow span the representation of formal object-making and something else, some other kind of social engagement?

JP: I hope they will be right. This idea that suddenly we are producing objects to be put on a shelf – like a Vitra miniature Eames chair – is quite laughable. Architecture is not about objects.

WM: Everybody seems to be speaking against the idea of curation. Is there anybody here who wants to stand up and defend it, or advocate for it?

OK: We are just saying that we need to define it.

MC: No, I'm saying I'm against it.

Ingrid Schroeder: Are we not speaking more about the argument about what we're displaying: whether we're displaying architecture at all? And the question is whether it is a sort of series of artefacts or whether it becomes a series of experiences. There's a fantastic comment from Massimiliano Fuksas in the first volume of *Architecture on Display* about the biennale being a continuous happening. But if we are indeed basically exhibiting a series of objects that are essentially retrospective, the idea of a happening is obsolete. So what do we give to a public that isn't architectural or professional, other than a setting for those happenings? And then, perhaps we're not really exhibiting architecture, but producing it on a small scale, which is quite a difficult problem.

SG: A good example of what you are talking about was the British pavilion at Venice this year, which was curated by muf and was fantastic. It was an event space and a happening space – and it wasn't displaying architecture. It was making architecture happen because it was a place where exchanges could take place. And there is a big difference, which I alluded to at the beginning, between art, as a thing that's exhibited, and architecture. Whilst I was very taken with Mark's critique with regard to the failure to achieve a relationship between audience and artwork in the Judd show, there's a different problematic with architecture. The traditional way of making an architectural exhibition is to display drawings and models, which, when you think about it, is quite ludicrous. If you're displaying a model at a fiftieth the size of the real thing and yet pretending it's the real thing, that is a big problem – it's not intuitively the way that viewers respond to it. I think that the muf presentation dealt brilliantly with that by creating something that wasn't an architectural model. It was a piece of the stadium for the 2012 London Olympics, and in bringing it to Venice …

Sarah Entwistle: It's a 1:10 model. And they're relocating it back in London, I think in a school, so it becomes a 1:1 element of the city. It has a life beyond the biennale, and becomes a site of production where there's a dialogue happening – a bit like what's happening now in this exhibition of Cedric Price, where this discussion is taking place. My question is, how did you and William and Brett choose the format for tonight, and what made you decide to close the doors and make it a private event when we're talking about public and audience and the exhibition being a site of experimentation and discussion?

Aaron Levy: There's a default tendency to envision the public as spectators, as excluded from the conversation. Perhaps we ourselves constitute a public as well – one that has the potential to imagine another public into being as the consequence of our address. Tonight's discussion was organised around the basic understanding that it is important to think together critically and creatively, with everyone sitting at the same table and with an opportunity to speak. The form that tonight's discussion has taken also reflects Bill's and my experience working in Venice, where we were quickly caught up in a rather spectacular economy of cultural tourism and display. Tonight's conversation is predicated on a more intimate and discursive model. Actually, John, would you like to speak to this question of intimacy? You were saying to me before that perhaps the consequence or even function of these biennales is to call our attention to the importance of holding on to intimate encounters?

JP: Not only encounters. I think that the most interesting moments of public gathering or assembly operate on the most dramatic levels of intimacy.

Otherwise, they are just fascist moments and not interesting. I don't know if I'm interested in intimacy, but I'm interested in the relation between the way people would perceive the world individually and collectively as subjects. I totally agree that exhibitions are modes of experimentation, but the problem I see is that, as such, they highlight how the architectural culture of 2011 is equivalent to the scientific culture of 1721. We haven't gone through the transition that reduced the world to the sliding ball of Galileo, where everybody had to look at the same object, the same model, through a perceived code. And what was important was not *what* you were actually looking at – this ball sliding down – but *how* you looked at it. With the discovery of something like thermodynamics, the mode of perception is no longer even important. Suddenly, you discover many other things, including the possibility of maintaining energy, and that's a completely different aesthetic idea. Architecture is not only decades behind, it also seems like we are stuck in pre-modern times, where we can only think of having a Galilean approach to the object. In the meantime, the world has moved on so much that the rest of the world considers this way of doing things irrelevant.

VN: Aren't there other examples? For instance, the Venice Biennale in 2006 with the French pavilion under Patrick Bouchain, where there was a French performance group inhabiting the space? I almost feel that the question of architectural display is irrelevant now. I don't think anyone discusses how to show a plan anymore. Maybe we have a privileged position because we're at the AA School, and we're allowed to explore ideas through very particular ways of seeing things, such as an audio exhibition. There is something really exciting about someone living in the space of the architectural exhibition. Actually, I think that a lot of architectural exhibitions today are about collaboration, moments of intimacy, the idea of someone making and sharing food, about talking and about people coming together. Those kinds of things are as important as showing work.

JP: I'm well acquainted with the complexity of architecture, yet it still operates exactly around an idea of, 'Look at the world like this.' There's always that hand showing you how you are to look at things – even in this exhibition, when you are discussing Cedric Price: the entire display is a reduced model of a Galilean experiment that tries to show that a feather and a lead ball are subject to the same variables. I'm suggesting that there are so many other ways in which we can operate in architecture today – we can discuss and perform, and we can activate aesthetic and political movements. The exhibition is just one of many agencies, and it's just one of many forms of practice, which is where I completely agree with Shumon: I find the very idea of discussing display as an exceptional or important condition irrelevant. Not because I aim to devalue it, but because today there are a multiplicity of practices.

IS: We treat the display of architecture as the recreation or the orchestration of an event in a setting. That's what architecture's doing pretty much all of the time, and I suppose I have difficulty with that idea. What I find interesting about Venice is that the biennale – particularly this year – has a particular relationship with the city. The way in which it's spread through Venice and begins to reflect on how the city displays itself is interesting: it enables us to begin to question the role of the institution as a site for the display of architecture or art. But I really want to question whether we should return to what almost seems like a grassroots approach of making architecture open to people, by saying, 'OK, if it becomes the site of an event, if it becomes a place where people can "interact", then it becomes valid as a way of describing architecture to the public.' I don't necessarily think that's true. I think people can enjoy the muf space, I think it was a fantastic orchestration of a series of events, something that muf does very well. But I don't think anyone outside of the architecture community recognised that was a 1:10 portion of the Olympic stadium that extended beyond the pavilion and defined how they organised the construction of the exhibition, etc. But I don't think that's necessarily the display of architecture, and I don't think that's necessarily the answer to the problem that Shumon brought up before.

WM: And what's that problem?

IS: Of us being somewhat behind: we're producing work in a very different way from artists. We're not producing for exhibition, we're producing to provide settings. We're in conversation with one another, and how do you extract that without being overtly didactic in the form of an exhibition? I think there's a problematic history here, in terms of a nineteenth-century ideal of teaching people to recognise culture. And this history is particularly acute when it comes to how we display architecture. Perhaps that has freed up a great deal when it comes to art, but I don't think the same applies to architecture.

MC: Maybe it would be useful to distinguish between art and architecture exhibitions. If one agrees that architecture is a kind of two-dimensional process of drawing and designing, then actually an architecture exhibition is normally what we call construction, that is, the form of exhibiting the design. I never find the term representation very helpful. Fine, call it architectural drawings or histories in bits and pieces – and maybe that's different from showing art objects. But if you think that through, you may get some idea of how you might do it in a general sense, but that yields something about the specific. With the Palladio exhibition at the Royal Academy, for instance, they produced an immensely good scholarly catalogue – indeed it's an indispensable text – but made the exhibition itself really boring. You're not going to get a better feeling of Palladio by having computerised walkthroughs of the buildings … that to me just seems silly.

WM: Why do you think this is? Is it because that's what the curators think the public would like to see?

MC: I think a lot of people are very dumb, and don't take this seriously: architects, artists and, above all, curators.

Léa-Catherine Szacka: I agree that in architecture the words curator and curating are overrated. I think it's more about creating an event, and in that regard it's particularly interesting how Paolo Portoghesi created an event with *Strada Novissima*. He also created a surprise in doing so, because no one had seen the Arsenale before. It's a wonderful space, and each time I go, every two years, I still think it's wonderful. I think the first time they showed it, it was really like a sort of happening. And maybe it's true that in architecture the biennale is something that you can do only once. A lot of the directors who featured in the first *Architecture on Display* book said, 'I would not want to curate two biennales in a row' – because I think you just do it once. For the same reason, it's interesting that a lot of curators in the book repeatedly go back to Portoghesi and *Strada Novissima*. Portoghesi had curated one exhibition before the 1968 biennale: on Michelangelo. So he wasn't a curator, per se. He didn't have considerable experience. Maybe curating in art is something that can be institutionalised, and that you can learn, but in architecture it's more difficult, because it's about something magical: you create an event, you create something.

Basar: It's probably impossible, but I think it's important to stress how often we're caught up in our amnesia, replaying certain moments. Yes, the art world has a slightly longer history with regard to terminologies of curation. But if you were to ask Harald Szeemann, he would never say that. He would refuse the term curator. Although he was technically, for us, the first independent curator,

112

the term didn't exist then. But we understand him to be a curator through what he did, by setting up and then leaving the Kunsthalle in Berne, then setting up his agency, etc. It also happened that air travel became accessible for everyone in the 1970s. You can't disentangle all of it, it seems to me …

> LCS: I think the word for curation is also interesting. In French you have *commissaire*, but you don't really have an equivalent to the English word curator. I found myself so many times trying to write it in French. But there is no equivalent.

MC: To take up Shumon's point, it's important that in English it has first of all a theological dimension. The term curation refers to that ecclesiastical function of taking care of souls. It displays here in an open character its moralising and improving character, which is what I think the latter-day curator is. How many times have you read interviews with people, where they start off with that dreaded sentence, 'What I think is important today is …' Every time you've seen that, don't you think the rest of this is not going to be worth reading? It follows as an iron law, communicated in some daft panel discussion concerning what is most important in the world. It's a new public daftness.

Genealogically, the term curator also clearly refers us to the historical structure of museums and galleries in the Anglo-Saxon and American world, where museums have traditionally had departments. At the British Museum, you had the department of Greek antiquities, and probably the department head was either called Head of the Department of Antiquities, or Curator. They weren't working all the time on exhibitions: they were looking after the stuff that was in their care. It was Thatcher who broke that system, by putting in Elizabeth Esteve-Coll as director of the Victoria & Albert Museum, in London, in the 1980s. She destroyed the institution's curatorial basis, and you can see how the rise of the modern curator is based on the destruction of the older system. She got rid of the link between particular holdings and expertise, so now anyone can be the head of fashion design, as long as they get enough people to come see it in a year, and have a handsome turnover for special exhibitions. I remember shocking people when I said the important thing about this gallery was how to get the number of visitors down. I was told afterwards it was the first time anyone had ever suggested it. The fact that it was too crowded was being used as an argument for the destruction of the Hayward Gallery – a building that we tend to love. There was a point at which they said it's getting too crowded, let's pull it down and do another one. No, let's reduce the number of visitors. It's a perfectly reasonable solution, but the avarice of a combination of the market, or the wish for popularity on the part of

Blairism, comes to the same unholy thing. Packing more people in is considered an absolute good. But in fact it's not. Curators are borrowers, they're basically art sub-prime mortgagers.

Basar: OK, but I'm going to contradict what I said earlier, following on from Mark's comments. I think it's important to go back to someone like Szeemann, and Hans Ulrich Obrist's book *A Brief History of Curating*. It is really worth reading because you realise that Carl Sandburg, Pontus Hultén, and the others, almost none of them came from an art background. They were specialists but in other fields, be it literature, physics, whatever, but the project of taking on an art institution was a cultural and ideological project of which an exhibition was a constituent element but not the most important. And that's really key. I do bemoan the professionalisation of both the curator and institutional managers, because that epistemological slippage is something we take for granted. That's what kept and made these institutions great places: you were never really sure what was going to happen next. And that seemed to be engrained in the DNA of the place. It is impossible now precisely because of the almost a priori nature of institutional decorum that is embedded in educating these characters, and in that sense it just becomes a kind of predestined endgame that comes down to things like health and safety. It's not that they're not important, but to somehow elevate them to the same kind of horizon... In the vacuum that's left by not really having ideologues leading institutions, things like that end up taking their place. And that's why I just don't understand the architectural community's sudden obsession with curating, or its jumping on the curating bandwagon. It seems to me that the effects of it are actually damaging.

WM: Do you think there's a way, perhaps by placing curation in quotation marks, of doing it in a creative and provocative way? Young people still open Storefronts. Is there any worth in doing that kind of project anymore?

AL: Another way to approach it might be to ask whether there are ways to be evasive towards the professional. If so, what would be those ways?

Basar: I'd hope that the impulse that a bunch of young 20-year-olds would have to want to start a space is perhaps the same impulse they'd have to start a magazine or an events night. The irony is that it's something that we need to continue. It seems to me that the Tate Modern or MoMA are only as healthy as the state of the new things that are happening. A healthy institutional culture is one that allows for that entire spectrum to happen and refresh constantly. Places like New York or London have an energy that leads me to think they will always constantly produce. I started a magazine 11 years ago, at a time when you could look on the book- and magazine shelves and find half a dozen independent titles, now there's maybe two hundred. It's clear we're in an age, certainly in the privileged half of the world, where overproduction is the standard and normative. What's so disappointing, particularly with a younger generation, is that what they aspire to doesn't seem to be much different from what people in their forties aspire to. Everyone's going for the same prizes, the same institutional positions. So that notion that you would kill your idols, or really try and change things, seems implausible. One of the most pernicious things, for me, is how art fairs have eclipsed biennales. Like you were saying, Mark, at least there's an honesty with private funding or an art fair that this is what it is. There isn't this duplicity, or this humanistic performance that it's something else. But you look at the lists of participants in the art fair and the biennale, and they're basically the same.

WM: In the art world, sure. But do you really think it's the same in the architecture world?

Basar: What is the market in the architecture world? In that sense Olympia's right, there are certain systemic differences between the two. But at the same time, why is it that Norman Foster gets Deyan Sudjic to write his biography for him? It's not benign that the Design Museum, in London, picks John Pawson to do its new interior and gives him a big show. Would it have ever given him a show otherwise? Of course not. Now they need to promote him, they need to raise his cultural status, etc. There's a sense in which institutions have always done that, and architecture curators are the means by which this happens.

Another addendum is the relationship between the curator and the art critic. There's been a shifty transposition of power between the authority of the art critic as career-maker to that of the curator and, of course, the gallerist. This represents a kind of collusion: at the end of every evening, at any biennale, they'll all be sitting around the same table and drinking the same expensive wine. It seems to me that there isn't a challenge being presented by the younger generation to this kind of power structure. Actually, everyone wants to be part of it and go to the same parties, and that seems to me a hallmark of our time. Until that changes, I don't see how anything else will change.

AL: If we've problematised the role of the curator in the way that we have in relation to over-production, bureaucratisation, even collusion, what are some of the remaining scenarios or methodologies that we should consider? Would there be one of refusal or disengagement? Would anyone at the table argue for non-production as a sort of practice?

Liam Young: I don't think so. If we're divorcing the art exhibition from the architecture exhibition, then perhaps it might also be important to divorce architectural display from exhibition. As Shumon said, most art comes into the world through the medium of the exhibition, but it's not the way that most architecture comes into the world. And that's not to say that most architecture comes into the world through development processes and building buildings on the street either. But it may be that this happens through film – it may be through the rewriting of seaside Florida as a Fordist utopia in the *Truman Show*, or the reimagining of Thamesmead South as a set for *A Clockwork Orange*. Equally, the medium may be the magazine or the book, or it may be the video game or the blog or the webosphere. Today the medium of architectural display is much more complex and nuanced, and that's an opportunity for a reinvestigation of the life of the curator beyond the domineering professionalism. The media through which we operate as designers have been opened up. The exhibition so often predicates the endpoint of our practice as the building or the physical object. But it's not – for there are different sorts of architects today in the same way as there are different sorts of artists and writers. And we need to be as dynamic in thinking about the way these things are disseminated around the world as we are in all these other kinds of disciplines.

Shumi Bose: I would like to second that: there's a much broader field of practice than we typically encapsulate within the term exhibition. When I think of exhibitions, I'm drawn to Mark's point of institutionalisation, and I want to understand what's providing the backing for an institution to stand behind a particular arrangement of work. We're not sure how far we ought to patronise this public, how far we ought to break things down and arrange things for them, or how it should be presented to this public ... those are the kinds of mechanisms that I'm trying to investigate when I go to an exhibition.

Olympia, you mentioned competitions before. This is something that is a very specific function of an architecture exhibition, which we can't parallel with an art exhibition. You're talking about having an architecture competition that would then be on display, and interact with and have an impact on policy. We've talked about other exhibition practices that try and expose the processes involved in the practice of architecture. And again that's separate from one that tries to recreate the use of architecture, say in habitation for example, or something that's trying to showcase a virtual rendering that you can occupy. These are disparate activities, and each of them requires a particular backing and motivation. I find it difficult to consider the exhibition as an encapsulating concept.

Beatrice Galilee: It's not just an expansion of the notion of curator that one finds today, but also the notion of an architect. The actual practices of architects today – particularly in London and in a recession – are wildly different from the kind of thing that would be exhibited in a formal exhibition space or in a museum. There is a fluidity between disciplines, and also a working with ideas and experimenting with forms of presenting these ideas and communicating their thoughts that is of interest to me. I think the discussion has moved on a bit, but I would contest that people still regard display as a valid concern. In our own space, what we're trying to do is provide a platform for ways of operating. It's nothing more pretentious or ambitious than that. It seems slightly naive but, well, we have a room, you guys don't really have anything to do, you don't really work, and don't really have any money and neither do we, so well, go ahead, and let's see what you can do.

VN: I think that picks up on something you were saying before. What is the new movement going to be? What's going to shake things up? I think it is actually the idea of event spaces rather than exhibition spaces. I think that collaboration is a very popular way of working now. It's not enough just to have an architect working on her or his own. You've got to be working, and preferably with a scientist, definitely with an artist. But I do think that, loaded and clichéd as it may sound, this is also the forefront. Maybe this will become a much bigger part of what we expect from an architectural exhibition, namely that they will be more about events or ideas. We've all now decided to give up on the idea of showing a plan or a model.

LY: I still think whether you call it an event space or exhibition space, whether it's in the Venice Biennale or a pop-up store in New York, it's still a mode of exhibition. But I also think we're potentially beyond a mode of displaying architecture that sites itself within a particular space in the city. The medium of display is more dynamic and diverse and transmedia. It has exploded into the world of glowing rectangles that we now occupy, including blogs. Students of mine are now operating within the video game industry and designing environments that people are occupying and inhabiting. Other guys are now working in the commercial industry and are developing a spatial practice, albeit through the medium of 30-second commercials and music videos. This, too, is a mode of display that places itself in a physical location. I think it is a mode of display that we should be engaging with and talking about in the same tone that we talk about a curated exhibition.

WM: Why should we be?

LY: It has much more force now, and it has much more of an audience. If one of the questions of architecture and display is about engagement, then these are the media through which most people are engaging with the media that we work with.

MC: Well, I just want to make a very simple point. It seems to me you have to start thinking about what the problems are that exhibitions are addressed to solving. I don't think there's an eternal necessity for exhibitions or something. If architecture is in some sense to us a source of knowledge, then it ought to be able to generate a type of argument, and maybe it's the type of argument that's not always best put in a book to be read by very few people. In the last 25 years, there has only been one major architectural exhibition, to my knowledge, that took the form of an argument and a polemic and was visited by a very large number of people: Prince Charles's

A Vision of Britain, in the late 1980s. You don't
have to recruit me to hate it, but it was basically
an architectural version of Hitler's exhibition
on degenerate art. It was vile, it was loathsome,
it was duplicitous, and it was entirely ignorant.
But it was extremely effective. The problem is
architects are impoverished figures at the level
of political calculation: they can't get out there
and deal with the problem. Are there examples
of revolutionary situations in which what's been
generated happens within the architectural
field? There's no need to pretend it's going to
take the form of an exhibition of architecture.

LCS: I think the point about controversy is interesting. If we come back to the last biennale, there
was not a lot of discussion and controversy. I think
it would be interesting in a year and a half to have a
biennale where architects are fighting. Let's really
have a discussion, because I think that's what has
been missing.

In the first volume of *Architecture on
Display*, Baratta says at the end, 'What is an architecture exhibition?' And in the interview Hans
Ulrich Obrist did at the last biennale he also repeat-
ed this question. He said there is not one answer,
and I think that's really interesting. I don't think
there is one way either. Each of these directors
of the biennale have tried a different approach or
direction. I think showing the process of architec-

ture is an interesting one, because it's interesting for the public to understand how you do architecture, but it's not the only approach.

IS: I wonder if it's interesting to understand how we do what we do?

LCS: I think it is.

Bose: I guess what you're saying is that there ought to be space for people who want to show those things. All I was saying was that when I look at architecture exhibitions, what I'm trying to discern is the agenda. Are they trying to show me how they do things? Are they trying to immerse me in the environment that they designed? I am not saying that I favour exhibitions that speak to the public in some way, only that I favour trying to understand what an architecture exhibition is.

Basar: One of the reasons I find 99 per cent of architecture exhibitions – and now books and magazines as well, and pretty much the whole culture of it – to be deeply boring is precisely the masturbatory way in which it is just talking to itself and each other. There is no dearth of space where architects wank each other off or stab each other in the back. In that sense I totally agree with Liam: it's interesting that if you really want to see how architecture speaks to a broader public, it's not in these domains. Whether it appears in the beginning of a James Bond movie or even home makeover programmes or wallpaper magazines, there are ways in which it does. I've always maintained that film directors understand architecture a hundred times better than architects do. Antonioni knows that the building is important not just because we look at the building, but because it's the backdrop against which we look as a couple fucks. I generally try and spend a lot less time with architects, particularly above a certain generation. They're so unbelievably narcissistic, as though the rest of the world doesn't exist, and shouldn't exist.

I think the term display is really interesting, because it's obviously much broader. It includes exhibition, various forms of representation and also presence. Display doesn't necessarily have to be representation. Actual presence is a form of display, so, in that sense, I think it's interesting.

VN: Are you really asking, 'What's the problem with architects?' And not, 'What's the problem with architectural exhibitions?'

Basar: Well, you can't really separate the two. Imagine we are having this same discussion, but we replace the word architecture with the word art every time. It would be the most nonsensical conversation. And that's the thing that just drives me nuts.

There's a sense in which art assumes it's already there, it doesn't need to have this ontological worry whether it's there or not. Why does architecture have to do that? Why does it have to be a profession in which things are either just for us or there's a public? There's always a multiplicity, there's always a plurality. It's the same in the art world. You have monographic exhibitions that are clearly there to help to construct the career and also the capital of the artist. At the other end of the spectrum you still have, thankfully, thematic and ideological shows.

One thing that hasn't really been mentioned today is that the modern curator, it seems to me, fits into a narrative of basic auteur theory. I was reading about André Breton and his whole notion of auteur theory, with the move from being a critic to being a producer. They actually did not have any ontological problem about this. In the art world the big problem is that curators are eclipsing artists, and suddenly artists feel like they have to protest like they're being diminished or something. But I do feel there is something like a good editor, who's editing a thematic anthology, or a good curator, who is arranging the exhibition. It goes back to Mark's point about the importance of having an idea or an argument. There is a sense in which I think the exhibition or the event can be the putting forward of a problematic in which people's work is a constituent element. For me that's still the most noble part of what it might be to be a curator.

OK: I have a specific example which maybe will open up the conversation, and which demonstrates the importance of having different spaces for different audiences. I don't know how much you followed in London the MoMA show called *Rising Currents*. It was a show that started as a workshop at PS1 in which different friends were selected by MoMA, five firms or so, and there was an intense process over a few weeks where they were doing workshops and pin-ups, etc. After a few months, it became a blockbuster exhibition for a wide audience at MoMA in Midtown. So it started in Queens and moved there. It was interesting how different the discourse and the conversation were, and how the different designers would act, within the PS1 context. What I liked about that process was the fact that this friction among the architects produced a different kind of work.

JP: What we are experiencing all around us, as Shumon was saying, are many attempts to find different discourses and practices. This morning Aaron was saying that there are a number of ways not just of engaging but also being entangled with institutions – entangled such that you cannot really distinguish whether there is an institution operating behind the project or whether there is a difference anymore between being in MoMA PS1 or MoMA in Midtown. I think that this idea of entanglement brings to mind an idea of cleavage. I am more and more interested in the distinction between the pedagogical mode, which I can attach somehow to art, and the non-pedagogical mode, which is constitutive of design. Design is non-pedagogical by its very definition. And I think that the enlargement of architectural practice to include display and all these other forms of entanglement is interesting. I would say that being complicit with different modes of producing very bad things in the world is interesting, because it is somehow creating a similar mode of entering and exiting, of being – or not being – pedagogical in design. It is like a grey zone that is forming around architecture, and I find that fascinating. And I would really like it to become grey matter – a little bit of intelligence inserted into that grey zone as well … more than just a process of institutional entry and exiting into bureaucracy.

MC: One could go a bit further, by almost proposing a thought experiment. I don't think architecture should have ever been a profession – I think it's a failed profession. It is absolutely clear that it should have been a trade union. That is to say, it should try to look after its members, and try to double the salaries of young architects. Everyone says that the strike weapon doesn't work anymore. Well, it would work against Norman Foster's office, given his deadlines. So if you experiment with that and just think for a moment, what would happen if architecture didn't have these grandiose pretensions that come from it being a profession? It's not even a political argument. It's just to invite people to speculate about how this question of exhibition and the presentation of knowledge would look if we were all suddenly institutionally framed in an entirely different way?

OK: I don't know what's the difference between a trade union and a profession ...

MC: Well you should. A trade union has a legal-based monopoly over a certain practice or knowledge. This is obvious in the case of doctors and lawyers. The problem with architecture is that it has never been able to define the object over which it should have a monopoly.

JP: What a trade union is, in classical economic terms, is a response to the division of labour. The division of labour calls for the unions to arise, and they are basically the ones who are resisting this division of labour. This is the interesting condition of this discussion – how it suddenly takes a weird twist with regard to the specialisation of the curator vis-à-vis the division of labour. It does not happen because things are now precarious and there is no money. So what, if we have no money. The function of the labour union is not to protect us from having no money but exactly the opposite: to re-conquer the condition of having knowledge and organising that knowledge. If there is a battle that architecture could fight, this could be at least part of it.

> Kari Rittenbach: I'd like to just speak to what you've been saying, John. If architects were a labour union rather than a group of 'professionals', then maybe the exhibition would be more discursive. Maybe it would be more about practice and how people work together. Whereas it seems like what we've been discussing here is the exhibition as a means of self-promotion and or of producing objects. I think Shumon was saying that every architecture exhibition seemingly has to prove that architecture is a field. But it seems to me to be more the case that every architecture exhibition has to prove that the architects involved have a monopoly over how architecture should be practised. A polemical exhibition about how different architects approach architecture could be more productive.

Jan Nauta: At some point we have to conclude that we are all completely fed up with the narcissistic way in which architects display either themselves or their work. I don't like the word curating. I think it has more to do with organising and facilitating, and it's a word I'd rather avoid. But it is, in a kind of almost violent way, the means by which we can participate in a realm of discourse. It gives us an opportunity to bring in voices, projects and things that create interesting clashes between different force fields and that, fundamentally, brings people together.

> Scrap Marshall: But is this architecture as a starting point, or as a finishing point? Mark has spoken about this before: 'Here's my research, then I'll rush you through all these projects', and all in five minutes. People actually have an argument that can start and finish in such a short time. Similarly, architecture exhibitions seem to cram it all in so quickly. I want to think of architecture instead as a starting point …

MC: I think there are other experiments that you could play with. What would an architecture school or an architecture exhibition look like if you banned images? I think a little iconoclasm, as a general practice, would be good. I have, much to people's horror, refused to show a single slide in 30 years. I regard myself as a critic of photography; I think graphic images are not a good way of explaining a project to someone – they're deeply misleading. The students, let alone the public, have been so completely corrupted into the form that they can't think without an image. It has become a kind of authoritarian thing: what they are going to get is the image, and they're not going to be presented with alternatives. It's a tyranny that nobody notices, but that doesn't mean that it's not a tyranny.

Conversation Four
Chicago

Graham Foundation for Advanced Studies
in the Fine Arts, Chicago, Illinois

*This conversation took place on 27 April 2011. It was
organised by Ellen Hartwell Alderman, Sarah Herda,
Aaron Levy and William Menking.*

Penelope Dean: We're at a moment in which we
need to inject more intelligence – indeed intellectual ambition – into work made today. Architecture
was historically allied with art as a symmetrically
strong discipline. What's happened since 1980 –
the 1980s being a key moment that needs to
be unpacked – is that architecture allied itself with
design – a general field. By design I don't just
mean the modernist aesthetic specialisations, but
an expanded definition of design that now includes
non-aesthetic fields. Through that shift, we have
a condition where architecture, as a discipline, is
allied asymmetrically with a profession, or a field.
I think that architecture's relationship with other
disciplines and fields has turned upside down.

Mark Wasiuta: It's interesting to begin with
the 1980s when thinking about the relation to

other fields. In the 80s architects were often accused of performing as artists, of extensive and illegitimate borrowing from art practices. Yet I don't think it was as simple as architects suddenly masquerading as artists. Historical architectural preoccupations were also responsible for the appearance of that work. Many architects in the 80s were reclaiming experimental practices from the 60s and 70s, or even earlier. One immediately thinks of radical American or Italian groups who pursued installations and exhibitions as forms of architectural production, and who found different venues for architectural events and more socially oriented practices. Yet I don't think 80s installation work was simply positioned against commercial practice or professionalism: installations were part of a growing repertoire of tactics and strategies that were played out in galleries and spaces that had appeared in New York and that were newly available to architects.

PD: I'm all for the public reception of architecture, but I'm glad the multidisciplinary project is over. This isn't a critique of the proliferation of spaces for exhibitions, it's a critique of the multidisciplinary project, which is about the hybridisation of fields, as distinct from a transdisciplinary project, which someone like Mark Linder would argue is about the importation of expertise or knowledge into one's field from another.

Tricia van Eck: For the *Universal Experience* exhibition in 2005, we invited Rem Koolhaas to completely take over the atrium of the Museum of Contemporary Art (MCA), in Chicago. The project had a totally interdisciplinary focus and it involved students in the construction of a map – the purpose of which was to figure out how a city like Rome was constituted through military forces and architecture, but also through roads. As people walked in, it completely changed the space. We also included one of Diller + Scofidio's suitcases in that show.

Jason Schupbach: Hold on a minute: tonight I've heard multidisciplinary, and I've heard transdisciplinary. And now Tricia has offered up the word interdisciplinary. Tricia, what's your definition of interdisciplinary?

TE: Looking at multiple media to constitute a space and a show. I guess the thing that I was interested in is what is an exhibition. How does one show and really explain architecture with historical perspective to a public who walk into a museum without prior knowledge about what they are going to see? You present it through multiple channels.

PD: So for you it's about modes of communication?

TE: Yes, but not necessarily modes that an architect may be an expert in.

Lisa Lee: For me, if Jane Addams didn't invent it, then Adorno did. The strength of anything inter-disciplinary, multidisciplinary, or whatever you want to call it, is that each discipline operates by its own logic. When you bring them into collision you see the limitations of each particular logic. The strength of the architecture exhibitions that have taken place at the Hull-House and Gallery 400 at the University of Illinois at Chicago (UIC) for in-stance, is the way we have brought in many critical discourses – whether they were from African-American studies, women's studies, or history – to comment on the architectural practices in question. I think that makes people uncomfortable, and it raises serious questions.

William Menking: You mean it makes the public uncomfortable?

LL: And architects. But I would like to go back to some questions that I have about the biennale and the question of criticality. A couple of years ago, Jim Elkins at the School of the Art Institute of Chicago asked what I thought was a really great question about biennales. It was mostly about how so many artists who are doing really powerful work are really questioning national identity, and raising serious questions about the ideological construction of nation and state and how it functions. Then the biennales come and they reassert national identity over and over again. I thought it was such a great contradiction and I'm wondering how architecture might function in this way.

Alexander Lehnerer: Perhaps this doesn't fully answer your question, but just two days ago I told my colleagues in Zurich that I just completed my fourth exhibition as an architect here in the US. And they said, 'Well, Alex, you have become an American now: you're not building, you're doing exhibitions.' So I suppose, from a national perspective, that this is what an architect does here in the US. People my age in Zurich, they do one competition after the other, not one exhibition after the other.

JS: That's shocking to me, and it's the opposite of what we hear at the National Endowment for the Arts (NEA)! People talk about how everyone has all of those opportunities in Europe, but that in the US there are not enough chances to exhibit their work, and not enough chances for exposure for young architects. There are so few exhibition spaces, so few journalistic venues left. So it's a shock to me that people in Europe would think that the US provides these opportunities.

Theaster Gates: Look, I just want to complicate things a little bit. From the outset of this conversation I see six hierarchies of knowledge – pedigree and institutional relationship, among them – particularly in what Penelope laid out concerning the death of the exhibition, or at least the way it was practised in the 1980s or 90s. In many ways, I think there is a kind of mimicry here. Maybe I'm accepting that there are moments when my art practice has architectural inclinations, and that these labels of 'I'm this' or 'I'm that' are problematic. People are often multiple things. I do think that I am rooted in something, but I'm also connected: I'm rooted in a creative practice that's expansive. And it's expansive enough to include the built environment as well as the cultural moments that play into the built environment. One of the challenges I hear is that there are different things at stake for different kinds of curators, professionals and practitioners. And I want us all to just admit that our stakes are different. This is an important and relevant question for how people can imagine themselves within the profession of architecture.

Mary Jane Jacob: To stay with what Theaster is saying, for all of us, our positions and practices emerge out of multiple things, so none of us like these pigeonholes. But I hear this categorisation thing mixing at the table with that recurrent amnesia thing. For me, it's really funny to hear that this is a moment of curating and curation. Because I remember the white paper of the art critic Michael Brenson in 1989, about the curator's moment, which came out of the biennale explosion. There is an amnesia that starts the moment you're born. How much you look back and how much you look forward relates to that ego place where we all are. We think it all started with us, and have to feel that we've invented something. To some degree, as part of an educational institution, you have that feeling because you're meeting the new generation every year. Maybe without that, we wouldn't be able to go forward or see something or feel that wonderful energy, excitement and vitality that we're doing something new.

I remember this question of nationalism being discussed in the mid- to late-1980s. We were very much looking at those national pavilions as something that we were stuck with. On top of that, the US pavilion was owned by the Guggenheim, and still is. It isn't even a national pavilion; in a way, it's a private pavilion. On the one hand, what we were doing was trying to keep Thomas Krens and the Guggenheim from owning the decision of national representation and picking the people who worked for their own marketing goals and collateral profit. At the same time, the elders, like Tom Messer or Martin Friedman, were saying that we had to really safeguard the decision of national representation from a political decision-making process. This was before the culture wars had arrived, so we were thinking that we were just talking museum politics, not real politics. And we had already witnessed a lot of experiments at that time. For instance, one year at the art biennale, different nationalities were to be found in each other's pavilions. One of the other dynamics that came up at the time, and which ties in with what you're talking about, Theaster, was the individual who has a hybrid identity. Was the Brazilian artist indigenous if her Brazilian background preceded colonialism, or was she Brazilian? Or what about the artist from another country who was born somewhere else and then migrated? What was their background? This is a condition we know well in America, but it was a newer condition for the art world. Today, maybe we've moved towards the issue of manifestation. The challenge is to make something manifest. To take up those questions of nationalism, community and self-identity that artists in that period of the 80s and 90s raised and which I still celebrate. I hope that never ends.

TG: You know, Mary Jane, what feels good about this is the idea that maybe there are multiple architectures, depending on the curatorial question or personality one might be interested in. Then there are those people who might be more interested in the spaces in between. At any point, when you say the word architecture, one could be talking about a theoretical or disciplinary practice that's rooted in pedagogy, or one that's absolutely its opposite. I'm learning this with my own art practice. One could call oneself an artist, but that means absolutely nothing anymore. And I think that the word architecture is confusing and problematic, in that it doesn't just constitute a structure but means passionately different things to different people. I have to respect that there are multiple acts of architectural and curatorial practice.

MJJ: Is that new to the field, or is this just a really good moment for the field, because it's not one thing and there's not that solidity?

PD: There are absolutely multiple architectures today.

MJJ: Have there always been, and we just shut the other ones out?

PD: There are certain conventions, techniques and histories that differentiate architecture as a discipline from other specialisations. Therefore, one has different ways of going about things. But there is still a common set of criteria that we can discuss across the discipline. I think the issue of a theme is problematic in architecture today. Thematising magazines – whether as curatorial or sustainable or whatever – is problematic because as a strategy it acts as camouflage. It allows a lot of insufficient work to be included in publications.

MJJ: Are you defining curating as the process of creating a theme?

PD: I'm talking about quality. I'm interested in quality because the key thing we have to discuss is how do we choose and how do we communicate to a public that a choice is important, that it's chosen for a reason and above another reason?

TE: So what do you define as quality? Because, in the 1980s, you said they needed to move up to a higher level. And now again you're saying quality. Quality is always a gatekeeper.

MJJ: Quality has very often been taken as the result of the thing that we're looking at. In the world of contemporary art, I'm a curator of process. The quality for which I'm looking, and which we might agree on, is a critical acuity: an intensity of looking at something. It's about how you present it and also how you engender a new thing out of a set of questions located within a particular practitioner whom you have chosen because of their quality of thought and capability. But the end result of the thing might not be very well done, because the process was stretched a lot. Maybe it was excellent and of high quality, but what you were grasping for wasn't located in that object at that time: be it a building, an exhibition, whatever.

JS: It's called taking a risk.

TG: What's great about this is that Mary Jane has marked a territory that says that what goes into an exhibition space ain't about the end object. This may be the kind of thing that the art-historical position was rooted in, and that she argues by virtue of her political, professional and intellectual position.

MJJ: Process is about seeking the form it should take, and in the end we may say the form is some other thing – something that despite our stretching what an exhibition can be, isn't exhibition-like at all. It may be a book, it may be a class and it may be this conversation.

JS: Can I throw a little wrench into this? Because this is the biggest challenge we have at the National Endowment for the Arts. We are legislated to fund projects that are excellent –

and this is exactly what you're talking about – so we always have to have experts in the room who can judge excellence.

MJJ: I know that line...

Sarah Herda: I think it's a great line actually.

JS: I struggle with this word, so this conversation is incredibly informative and interesting to me. I completely agree with you that we love the risk and that the end product could be inconclusive but the process could be wonderful. Process is just as much of an art form as the product.

LL: But it's not just any process.

JS: How do you judge process? How can you determine – and this is a question I always have – whether or not the process is amazing? That the process is risk-taking enough, and expands the field, and pushes the field forward enough? How does one judge that?

MJJ: You judge it by the investment in that process. We could quantify it in time, the in-vested stake of the people who are there, the background of the people you call to the table, and also how you cultivate that process. There are processes that we know and there are real standards regarding process: who you bring to the table, what system you go through and how much they care about that. They may have a great background, but how much did they really invest in this, into the stakes of the unknown, into this leading somewhere? One can also judge them on their openness, because otherwise it isn't going to be a process. And then there is, of course, that very important other element, which probably doesn't fit into the culture of the National Endowment for the Arts, and it is trust. You have to trust that process. And not just in some sweet way like it's nice to trust people. How do we get to an innovative idea? Not by being an implementation process, but by being a discovery process.

SH: But I also think that to have a productive process, you need disagreement. You need people who have conviction and who are committed to their cause, and position, and idea. I also believe that important ideas about architecture don't always come from architecture. The idea of curating or creating programmes about architecture – whether it's a funding programme or an exhibition programme – can come through different voices and positions. You can have an institution that has one ideological purpose, but I happen to interpret my institution's mission in terms of boundaries. It's all about edges.

PD: But Sarah, I think this is where quality is really important. Just because a field expands, doesn't mean it's an advance. One has to have criteria.

SH: That's why I think you never can lose sight of the fact that it's completely subjective. Your interpretation of quality and mine – I'm sure they are completely different on many fronts.

LL: How about if the curator's job is not so much to judge quality, but to create an exhibition in which – and this is what I would argue we do at the Jane Addams Hull-House Museum – the visitor comes in, and they don't just consume content but they become politicised subjects. They don't just see something or some object, but rather their own subjectivity. So it's not about the subjectivity of the curator or the subjectivity of the object, it's about the viewer's subjectivity as they come to see the objects in your museum. That's how I would judge quality.

MJJ: Look, it's not that process totally enables artists. I don't want to put it in that hierarchical way, but I think it is an approach that allows something to happen. Curators with anything that could be construed as a partner relationship give artists the room to breathe. I was quite taken aback when some amazing artists would explain that curators sometimes use the word permission, which seemed to me to be so much about an authoritative stance. They would say, what you do in curating is give permission. I'm totally uncomfortable with that. And then I understood that, of course, we don't have permission very often to do things that are really quite natural, like think, speculate, come up with something else, bring a landscape architect into an artist team, etc.

MW: The notion of adjudicating quality seems slightly bizarre to me, and maybe not the most productive way to approach or to read curating. It risks echoing the Good Design programme through which MoMA in New York once attempted to foster a certain kind of audience and certain sensibilities, or tastes – an agenda of discerning, separating good objects from bad objects rife with suspect and moralising claims. But I am interested in the related question of how – through what terms – should we assess, discuss and evaluate, if not adjudicate, architectural exhibitions? This question might be motivating Bill's and Aaron's project on the Venice Biennale. At the very least the current discussion in architecture promises to make this a more important, informed and critical issue.

MJJ: Public. This is a word in our vocabulary now.

PD: It's a form of disciplinary laziness to put things under categories – for instance, that the next hot thing is curating.

SH: I want to complicate that. I think there's also an awareness right now that these things matter in the field. In certain ways, they have not had a lot of attention previously.

PD: I disagree. There's so much written about the aims of curating exhibitions.

SH: Actually there's little to no literature about architecture exhibitions. For those of us who do it, it is an interesting moment of trying to define the field. I think our roles in the field are being codified for the first time. I don't see that as laziness.

PD: I think this is symptomatic of something going on in architecture right now. There are a number of terms that are prolific, for example sustainability. I would put curating into that landscape. I'm not denigrating the practice of curating, but I have a problem with the way it is packaged as supposedly new content.

MW: I know that it is being discussed more, but I'm very curious about where you see it being packaged?

PD: I'm disinterested in thematised publications in general. For instance, if you look at *Architectural Design* or at *Volume*, every single issue requires a theme to organise its content. I think this is a form of intellectual laziness. For me the problem is the thematising of the curatorial field, not the field itself.

SH: I think that these themed publications, such as the *Log* issue dedicated to curating, are an important step, just as Henry Urbach's book on installation architecture, which will come out soon, is creating literature about the field. I think that's important, and not at all lazy.

MW: I would add that an ambition for these projects would be to ensure that it doesn't become a theme or trend, but rather that it becomes a more critically, historically and politically engaged practice.

JS: Thematising is a representation.

Alexander Eisenschmidt: What I find really funny and a little bit strange in this conversation, because I'm not a curator, is that we are talking only about the idiosyncrasies of the curator, and not the architect who is exhibiting something. This discussion resembles the discussion between architects and urban designers, wherein curators are to architects as urban designers are to architects, because in urban design it's the same issue of curating architecture in the city. However you want to call it – whether it is to curate or simply to bring stuff together, about single works of architecture or something larger – the best urban designer is the one you don't see. And, for me, the best curators I've been working with are those I don't see in the end. They frame a project, but somehow, just as a good urban designer does, they are not trying to plan everything, but to let things emerge. If we had this discussion at the end of the last century in Europe, I think we'd be having a similar conversation concerning what the role of the urban designer should be. It's also funny that, when you thematise a conversation like this, it always starts with a privileging of the present as a great moment – but I don't know whether this is a great moment.

MW: I don't know if it's a great moment either, but it is a moment of scrutiny. I teach a course in the Critical Curatorial and Conceptual Practices programme at Columbia University. The students were asking recently why architecture is currently so concerned with curating. It seemed right that this was addressed more as a historical question than as a valorisation of recent curatorial practices.

SH: I don't want to inflate or devalue the role of the curator, but I think that the important thing is the exhibition itself, and the site of the exhibition. Often what is missing in discussions of curation is the work itself.

LL: But don't you think it's about the perception of power, and the ability of an individual to challenge the power of an institution? Tricia, your name is so attached now to the *Without You I'm Nothing* exhibition at the MCA. Your curation of this particular show has challenged the institution to which you belong.

AE: Is that still a discussion? As a curator, it's still an issue to challenge the institutional? It strikes me as amazingly old-fashioned.

LL: That institutions have power and that they want to wield it over individuals?

TE: I'm here in the institution that Mary Jane challenged, and I'm still challenging the same exact thing.

LL: Right, that has always been the role of individuals in society. It's not like you ever reach a moment of liberation, or like the first generation of feminists achieved it and so I'm not going to have to do anything. The issue is that, as curators, as individuals, as parts of institutions, we're constantly engaged in trying to redefine the public sphere, in trying to redefine the public good, in trying to redefine what an institution is. An institution is not just a static thing, so we're always going to be pushing up against that. I don't think it's new, but it certainly is our task. And people who don't do that, sort of fail.

MJJ: Theaster, do you think you're curating Dorchester Projects, or is Dorchester curating you?

TG: It's curating me. But I do think that there is a way that there might be a kind of practice – maybe even if you just resisted the word curator – that could help enable certain kinds of emergences. I'd like to go back to a couple of these points that Penelope raised, which are really interesting to me. I felt that the word 'lazy' was really important, and laziness in relation to knowledge stewardship and these things. I wanted to put out the word popularity, and I think part of the challenge is that lazy people can be popular. Earnest people are quiet, and are about knowledge, and they are self-possessed. They do the work while the lazy people, who are the charismatic ones, reap the benefits. Maybe part of the obsession with the word curator, part of the reason why people in the architectural community are obsessed with the idea, is because the curator gets to be the most popular person in the exhibition. I'll give you an anecdote. I just joined an architectural team with Jeanne Gang, which was just selected for an exhibition at MoMA. The selection committee kept saying to the three of us: 'So what's going to be here? So what will we see?' There's been all this rigorous thought about a conceptual framework for the project and we were ready to tell them all this. But at the end of the day, there was also a space and we had to deliver some things and those things had to fill some 600 square metres. I'm talking about objects, not processes.

TE: Back to the 'show me'.

TG: I feel like the way that I've learned about architecture was not through museums. It was through books, and I've enjoyed that relationship with architecture. It was really helpful, and I feel like architects were able to advance the practices of architecture through those books, and through the smart people writing about them. And so I'm curious about other forms of curatorial practice, especially the book. I think that the book has been an important museological platform for the advancement of the field.

SH: Publications and exhibitions are modes of communication. When I was younger, I thought I wanted to be an architect. Then I realised that exhibitions and publications were the moment something became public, when it was communicated and therefore had the potential to change the field. And at that moment, as a 20-year-old working in an architectural bookstore, I decided that I didn't want to be an architect, but that I wanted to work in architectural publications or exhibitions. Exhibitions are an opportunity to produce work. It's about working with someone to realise a project, and the exhibition is a site in which to realise a new project. I think that exhibitions and publications – and I say this knowing that there are a number of institutional directors at the table – enable the construction of a free space. There are risks involved, there are high stakes, but the opportunity is to construct a forum for the expression of ideas, and to hold on to the possibility of failing or succeeding, and not knowing what the metrics are going to be.

LL: And it's also about reaching a different public. And the thing about exhibition practices, if you are a public institution and you're not just showing it in your house, for example, is that you have an obligation to the public. Mary Jane, you were saying the Hull-House has a different kind of history to other kinds of institutions – well, I would challenge that and say of course we do. The thing that's exciting about curators and great exhibitions is that they can be very self-reflective about the public they are addressing. As all the great queer theorists and the Michael Warners of the world would say, a public just doesn't exist: you have to address it for it to come into being. And how you address it is very important. Because that's where there is the opportunity to create a new kind of public.

Aaron Levy: Lisa, like you, I find in Theodor Adorno's writings a body of thought that's emblematic of the conditions we all find ourselves in today. One of the particular things I take from his work is an understanding of how complicit we all are with the very structures we are trying to work through. Apropos of this conversation, it's not just that curators are able to cultivate and engage publics, they're also completely marked by the institutions they find themselves in. Far from being hip progenitors of alternative publics, they're compromised figures. And the biennale for me is emblematic of all of that. It's not exceptional at all, and in fact it's emblematic of a larger cultural condition. I was wondering, is the curator for you, picking up on what Sarah was saying, one who cultivates free spaces, or is the curator the most compromised of all figures?

LL: I don't think there's a spectrum of compromise in that way. I think the curator, and I hate to take such a critical-theory-Frankfurt-School line, makes the contradictions obvious. The curator is not outside of any kind of stream of whatever is happening at that moment. We all move along in that stream, and there's a little window of opportunity to make that obvious, and to question and challenge it: sometimes this happens, sometimes not. The issue is that it has become so banal in our everyday discourse: the curator is like the person who works at Gap, who is curating the T-shirt collection, and that kind of thing. But that is also so illuminating, because it shows the commodification of what curators are doing, and who their public is, and what they're trying to do.

JS: Perhaps this is why people are obsessed with curators right now. There is so much informal art happening, and it's in fact something we're having trouble with at the Endowment. Not trouble, necessarily, because we're excited about it, but we have to deal with it. There's this explosion of informal artists and design and stuff that is happening, and we want experts to tell us what's good. And the thematising of these developments is a sort of storytelling, it's the simplification of complex issues into something like, 'Just tell me that's great, tell me exactly why it's great and cool. I just want to be able to talk about it with my friends at a dinner party.'

LL: But maybe that's not your responsibility as the head of a national organisation that is supposed to think about the common good, and be inclusive. You shouldn't be relying so much on experts to have a vision. You should perhaps be setting the standards, setting the vision of what a national organisation would be. That would be my same argument for a vision of what a public institution might do, versus what a private foundation might do. You should be responding and responsible.

PD: Jason's agenda, if I understand it correctly, is excellence in the field. So the question is, who are the people who can assess excellence? His model, right now, is a collection of specialists. If specialists can't do it, then who can?

LL: I'll give an example. I work a lot with radio, and we get radio grants and all these kinds of things. It's generally understood that Ira Glass is excellent in the field of radio documentary. So every time he applies for a grant, he always gets it. Now the issue is, should we continue to fund the aesthetic of Ira Glass because he's excellent, or should we as an organisation try to be proliferating multiple stories, multiple forms of discourse? And we should. But if you were to constantly ask us the question of who's the most excellent, you will always end up with Ira Glass.

TG: A monopoly!

SH: But I don't agree with that. I think that excellence is subjective, and that excellence is a really refreshing way to evaluate work, because it's through your lens and so it's about who you put at that table.

JS: And we make an effort to include the people who would see excellence beyond what some other people might think of as excellence.

TE: But what's the difference between excellence and quality? It's that same question. And it's difficult when fields are often changing and you're at the edge of that field that is changing. Like Mary Jane said, it's often difficult to judge in the middle of the process. It's hard to determine what is an excellent process.

LL: When Jane Addams came to Chicago, she had a vision of what was excellent and she wanted to make it accessible to the immigrants, to as many people as possible. She had a definition of what good taste was. The very first story she writes about is when she invited Italian immigrants into her home, and she thought what was good taste was her standard meal of overcooked meat and potatoes. And the Italian immigrants said no, let us make you something. And she wrote a beautiful letter to her family that said they had the most incredible meal. They boiled tomatoes, and they added meat and boiled it, and then they poured it over copious amounts of macaroni. Now this was her first taste of spaghetti Bolognese, and the immigrants also were so astounded because she had such a beautiful house, but not one head of garlic, because of course if you're a privileged white person you're not having garlic in your house. Jane Addams was astounded and she went on to realise that her definition of good taste was limited, much like the Italian Renaissance paintings that she hung on the wall and that eventually gave way to paintings by Mexican migrants and pottery that was made by the local community. The evolution of excellence in her life is interesting.

MJJ: But now let's come back to the Jane Addams Hull-House Museum. So you have criteria: you hope that people are not just consuming content but are also being moved to do something. Do you have some examples you could share with us, and also some evaluation of exactly what change looks like and how you do that mission excellently?

LL: Many of our exhibitions are community curated, which means inviting a whole set of other voices to the table. And it means realising that whatever topic, subject or object you hope to display, you may not be the expert in it. So curation is recognising that moment when you don't know what is excellent. And change is more grassroots, it isn't a top-down change – that's what Jane Addams said.

MJJ: But is the change within the way you do exhibitions? Or is the change in another sphere that you're aiming to reach in the social situation?

LL: It's in both, because exhibitions are sites for the creation of knowledge.

MJJ: In your experience, have you seen exhibitions affect social situations?

LL: I would say yes. We have an exhibition now on the prison-industrial complex, which raises issues of abolition in the Civil War period and also the issues of prison abolition today. 30,000 people come to our site. And those who participate in this exhibition do so by writing a card to somebody who's on death row, and they are thinking about these issues.

MJJ: I trust that it makes a difference, and I've been there. But do you have demonstrable examples? Because there are artists and architects and others who are working in procedural ways to actually see that change happen. Have you seen that happen? Is that something that your institution does as an outcome of its curating? It's not just OK that people are moved, and they do something. And I'm not belittling it, but that is, of course, the art museum mode: that we see a work of art and we're changed, and it makes a difference. And probably everybody at this table has had that, and that's good, but are there some things that are demonstrable from the social agenda? Particularly at the Jane Addams museum, which represents a certain intersection within this world of architecture and urbanism, because Jane Addams changed the city.

WM: You don't think that sending these notes to prisoners is a means of enacting change?

MJJs: No, that hasn't changed any laws.

LL: Why would laws and policy be the goal? Most of what Hull-House accomplished was before women even had the right to vote. And so cultural change was what they were trying to effect.

MJJ: But Jane Addams changed laws.

LL: Not only.

SH: I think we are talking about metrics here.

MJJ: Yeah, I'm looking for the evaluation of it.

SH: I'm very suspicious of certain conventions of evaluation.

MJJ: But I think we could own it and do it well, because what you do makes a difference.

SH: I don't think that the number of people who visit an exhibition means that it was successful or led to more change.

MJJ: But we do have to be clear on the goals, in order to assess exactly what is the quality of what we're doing.

JS: This is a huge issue right now in Washington, the metrics of how you measure your investments. We put on an exhibition, this many people came, and therefore there's quantity. But this is not good enough anymore. It's outcomes now that everyone cares about, which are enormously difficult to measure in the arts and in design.

MW: There are so many struggles that have been identified here – the struggle between the bureaucrat and the historian, for instance. The terms by which an historian might evaluate success is most likely to be different to the success of numbers. Barry Bergdoll pointed out the other day that almost nobody saw the International Style exhibition. And so it failed in terms of quantity of visits, but succeeded in almost every other form of evaluation. If, as Lisa's project hopes, curating might produce newly politicised subjects, and as Aaron reminded us, curators are constrained, even compromised, by the politics and expectations of their institutions, we might expect exhibitions to be sites of even more extreme struggles and conflict.

TE: Museums want to know what the public are going to see. They're not concerned about the experiential, they're concerned about what they are going to show their visitors. And that's a fundamental problem.

MJJ: But it's also about an anxiety that locates the object as something that resolves the complexities within this project.

TE: Because the object is market-driven, and we locate things in terms of objects. We don't talk in terms of the experiential, and that's why we can't articulate how a public views an exhibition. We don't understand anything outside of objects. We can say that we experienced interesting things, but we don't know how to articulate them except when we have an object. And that's the fundamental problem with architecture biennales and architecture shows. How do you project the work? Do you put a facsimile up, or a photograph?

> MW: Harald Szeemann first intended that *documenta* 5 would not be an exhibition of projects, but an exhibition of events. He then abandoned that approach, claiming as a reason that the 'event character' of the exhibition demanded 'optically impressive' experiences. In short, the exhibition comes with certain optical expectations that if not met, would not produce an audience. And so the question is whether or not the optical 'event character' produces the audience. This is exactly what you are up against.

TE: So, is quality when you can deliver opticals and experiences?

> LL: It's resonance and wonder.

AE: One curates an exhibition because it's about putting forward ideas and pushing the boundaries of the discipline – so it's always projective. But we are talking here about process-driven art and about challenging the very institution that we're working within, and I think architecture actually has moved beyond that. Architecture did it already.

SH: I think that all directors, all of us in these positions, have to change the institutions we're in. If we didn't, you wouldn't be at this table.

AE: I understand this as a way of curating architecture, too. I do think the question that emerges in the first part of *Architecture on Display*, of whether architecture can be exhibited, is a strange one, because ultimately architecture as a practice is not this thing we're in, but the drawing of it. It's by definition a thing that actually always projects forward. I understand that we have to challenge the institutions we're working within, but I don't think that this is the primary goal out of which disciplinary directions can emerge. Diller + Scofidio challenged the discipline, but it was also always a way for them to put new ideas into the field, rather than just work against the very thing they're working within.

SH: But I don't think challenging is working against. The mission of all these institutions that produce architecture exhibitions, that create this space of production, creativity and interpretation, is change. Change is intrinsic to all of our institutions, if we choose to enact it.

MJJ: Just remember amnesia. People whose institutions you inherited, and who you think never came from change, had their own battles and changes.

AE: But shouldn't architecture be the focus, not the institution?

Aaron Levy: Can we go back to Diller + Scofidio's project *Back to the Front: Tourisms of War* for a moment? They looked at how tourism and war are intertwined, and explored the mediation of war in contemporary society. Alexander, you spoke of the role of the exhibition in positing or displaying new ideas, and I would take issue with that. It's about being implicated by somebody else's ideas, and finding in the exhibition the possibility of coming to terms with and critiquing the societal conditions in which one lives. I say that as one who, like many of you at the table, is committed to advocacy and thinking about exhibitions as social processes. But there's always a danger in instrumentalising exhibitions in the name of outcomes. In fact, it's indebted to an economic logic, and I wonder if the question should be, how can we make sure not to instrumentalise exhibitions? I've spent the past year working with non-governmental organisations including the International Peace Institute and the United Nations University, to bring together diplomats and statesmen with philosophers and others to engage in conversation. It would be completely problematic and presumptuous to think that the outcome of this, however extraordinary those conversations may have been, will be a measurable geopolitical shift. But it would also be naive to think there's not something incredibly powerful about the idea of a conversation.

AE: Wouldn't you agree that you're curating ideas?

AL: Sure.

MJJ: But you're doing real evaluation at the same time. I'm not a metrics person, believe me, but reflection is the evaluation, and the research is the evaluation. And that's what *Architecture on Display* is about and what your work is grounded in, and that is the effect that you'll have on other people.

AL: But that work almost always comes after.

TE: It's interesting how so much of the Venice Biennale is pure practicality. It's like thinking, 'I have 30 days, what the hell do I do?' And you have to summon the will and just do it, as opposed to really getting the writer to compose.

JS: It wouldn't be fun if there wasn't drama.

TE: But it's this essence of curating that all the theorists completely forget. All the time, I have interns who say, 'Oh, you put that painting on that wall to signify what is the most important work in the show.' No, that was the only wall that painting fitted on! That's the practicality. In your project, Bill and Aaron, or with regard to the past directors of the Venice Biennale who you interviewed, it's, 'I couldn't get things delivered in time because of the boat shipment. And so we didn't have the funds to ship these works, and that's why I showed that one.'

SH: But I think those conditions apply to any space.

TE: But to talk about curating you need to talk about these kinds of issues. You can have your themes, and you can have your ideas, but in the end you have to get it done.

AL: Lisa, can you speak about whether the soup kitchen is a curatorial practice or project? I'm asking because I actually think it's a far more interesting form of practice than most of the 'exhibitions' I normally encounter. I'm interested in whether it's even important to you to frame it within a curatorial discourse.

LL: I do think it is. Basically, the soup kitchen takes place once a week in the residents' dining hall, a historic space of the Hull-House museum. We bring in farmers, food scientists, community members and scientists to talk about food justice issues. And we serve a delicious bowl of organic soup and bread, and there's conversation. So it's a communal meal that happens at the table. We also have an urban farm that we run, where we grow much of the food and we bring it in and serve it. The process itself of curating the soup kitchen has been a process to excavate our own history of the site, to rethink our role of what it means to be a public institution. To be a museum is, I think, a curatorial practice, but it's also because perhaps I have a different definition of what a curator does. It's a thick description maybe, but it has to do with a radical democratic practice, and so for me I'm interested in the earlier discussion of someone who is lazy. Laziness is when you are not consumed by your own identity, you're not advancing your own, and you're not hustling.

TG: What's exciting to me about the soup kitchen are the lay personalities related to it. Also, what Lisa brings to it is a set of curiosities and interests that is separate from the field of curatorial practice, maybe, or some accumulated set of presuppositions about curatorial practice.

MJJ: It's very related to artistic practice.

TG: You know, there are moments when artists act as curators. In this conversation about the architectural curator, architects themselves might have an innovation that could be much more successful than an architectural historian, say, who has the charge of always reflecting on great movements of architecture. Maybe from the ground up, an architect who's actually engaged in his or her own practice and involved with his or her drinking buddies could have this other kind of emergence that could be fruitful for architectural history. And so, what I'm excited about are all the folks who are not deemed curators. I would never call myself a curator. I feel kindred with Lisa, in having a particular set of positions, and just wanting to put those positions out there. The position might be a certain form of democracy, and in fact I'm not going to curate that.

SH: What's maybe a little obnoxious is the privileging of a curatorial position. But let's not be mistaken, there's no display of architecture without curation. So, in fact, it's a partnership; it's actually a relationship.

TG: Another thing I keep hearing tonight is an ongoing conversation about the way in which architecture relates to its professionalisation. And maybe you feel that artistic practices can resist this and still be successful, whereas architecture has a kind of professionalisation that artistic practices have resisted.

MW: I'm interested in where the boundaries are drawn between art and architecture, especially in relation to questions of resistance. Returning to how the lazy curator was earlier opposed to the diligent artist we could add the counter example of art practices as models of laziness. One reason the *flâneur* becomes such an important figure in the nineteenth century is that at some level he resists modernity and modernisation; he resists the mechanisation of his subjectivity. Like the *flâneur*, the artist has often been identified with potentially disruptive forms of laziness. Paul Lafargue and others associate laziness with resistance. Following this notion of laziness, I would ask how architects and curators could learn to be more lazy?

MJJ: I'm not comfortable with this lazy thing. I haven't met any artists who are lazy. I think it's denigrating to the artist.

PD: You need to separate lazy production from lazy thinking, because those figures who produce less are not necessarily lazy thinkers.

MW: The endlessly cited reference is Bartleby the scrivener, whose refusal is emblematic of this type of laziness.

AL: Perhaps what you find in Bartleby though is not laziness, but disengagement? Theaster, I was interested in that moment you shared with us about your experiences at MoMA: why didn't you disengage at that moment when you found yourself faced with a definition or an expectation of practice that wasn't necessarily what you saw as yours?

SH: But is that disengagement? I think that's actually about taking a position. Taking a stand is a form of engagement.

TG: There was a moment when they asked what would you do, and I said, well, if we get Cicero, Illinois, then what we'll do is in Cicero, Illinois. And how will MoMA respond to Cicero?

TE: What did they say?

TG: I think they liked the idea that the work would actually live somewhere other than the gallery.

LL: But let's not confuse the fact that they liked it for different reasons than you proposed it, or liked it yourself. That's not bad.

MW: You also have to understand that 'they' doesn't necessarily mean what you might think in this context. 'They', in this project, refers to invited curators and panelists. Their identification with the museum might be quite tentative.

TE: But they're still chosen. Those people are chosen by the museum for that very reason.

LL: And in a way, it is a tactic of the museum to use these temporary experts, or the NEH, or the NEA, to diffuse the sense of who 'they' are.

MW: I understand, but what I'm questioning is a flattening of the employee and the institution. There is often a more complex relationship than is immediately apparent. Employees, curators, directors, invited guests – all may be guilty of quiet subterfuge, of working against or using an institution for other ends, towards a counter project.

TG: To answer your question, Aaron, as to why I didn't resist more in the moment: I think I didn't resist because there's a part of me, and a part of my artistic practice, that wanted to be aligned with architecture through this cultural institution. The art practice had traversed through the cultural institutions and finished, and I was like, 'Let's do something else.' There was a way in which I wanted to see how flexible this nuanced practice or thinking about the house could be. How could we think about the house as a sculptural practice, a political practice, an architectural practice, a physiological or spiritual practice, etc.? How could we think about the same thing and just move through these varying systems? That felt, to me, like an art practice.

LL: But for you, don't the people who see Dorchester as 'just a project' represent a certain kind of privilege? You've talked a lot about this, but you cannot see it this simply, because as a black man working in Chicago, Dorchester will never be 'just a project'.

TG: It ain't just a project.

LL: When I hear the sense that architecture has moved beyond a set of issues, I think that certain architects are privileged to move beyond a certain set of issues, just like certain artists are. Certain people who work at museums are, but not everyone is allowed to.

SH: But I would actually slightly disagree with that. I don't think that it's only because Theaster is a black man working in Chicago.

TG: Thank you, love.

SH: I think you can make decisions as a black man working in Chicago that would be very different from the decisions that Theaster has made. I don't think that gives a complete definition of what his practice is.

TG: What's really great about what you guys are saying is that, for the architect, one comes bearing more than just their architectural practice. I think that one could be engaged both in a theoretical discourse about architecture, and in a studio practice where you think about buildings and you're invested in making buildings. As you complicate the set of things that you're interested in, you also adapt or adopt these other things. What you end up with is a trans-specialisation that's beyond this rarefying hyper-specialisation.

PD: I think hyper-specialisation is very bad. The green architect, for instance, is a hyper-specialist who specifies the application of technological products produced in other fields. That figure is no longer, in my sense of the word, an architect. By becoming so specialised, he or she has left the field.

TG: Maybe what I'm interested in, then, is a more holistic architect, who's concerned with the future and at the same time with old technologies. There might also be the kind of architect who is an opportunist; who knows how to operate better than other architects. For instance, by associating my practice with these words that people in the federal government would use, I could better advance my architectural practice. And at least it would be seen in the world. Maybe these people are more advanced in how they use the tactics or resources available to get an idea out. Let's say that I was a potter, who then became a self-described contemporary artist or a conceptualist. These words don't mean anything particularly different to me one way or another, as I would be doing the same work. But there are more resources.

TE: As an architect?

TG: Yes, as an artist. I keep asking us to declare the stakes because there are some architects who enter the profession to make money. Others want to make a change – and that's their thing. So we end up back at the issue of belief, and how we come to these things. I keep wanting people to just declare why they're in it.

Contributors

Shumon Basar is a writer, curator and educator. He co-founded the independent publishing/event collective Sexymachinery, is the architecture editor of *Tank* magazine and co-directs the curatorial/ design group Newbetter. He also teaches at the AA and the Royal College of Art, London.

Martin Beck is a conceptual artist who draws from architecture, design and popular culture. He has had numerous solo shows and is the author of *half modern, half something else* (2003) and, with Julie Ault, of *Critical Condition: Ausgewählte Texte im Dialog* (2003). He is also a contributor to the Vienna-based *Springerin* magazine.

Aaron Betsky is the director of the Cincinnati Art Museum, and in 2008 he was director of the 11th Venice International Architecture Biennale. He has published more than a dozen books on art, architecture and design and teaches and lectures about design around the world.

Shumi Bose is an editor, architectural writer and researcher based in London. She works at Afterall, a research and publishing organisation based within Central Saint Martins College of Art and Design, and teaches history and theory of architecture at the AA.

Matteo Cainer is an architect and a curator. He is an associate professor at the (ESA) Ecole Spéciale d'Architecture in Paris. He was also assistant director to Kurt W Forster in 2004 for the 9th Venice Architecture Biennale.

Sam Chermayeff is an architect at SANAA and a guest professor at Dia Institute of Architecture, Dessau. He has been the project architect for the Serpentine Pavilion, Derek Lam Flagship Store, Torre Neruda and has won several prizes including the first prize for the Bauhausarchiv Berlin extension.

Beatriz Colomina is an architectural historian and theorist who has written extensively on questions of architecture and media. Beatriz is the founding director of the programme in Media and Modernity at Princeton University.

Peter Cook is the founder of Archigram and a former director of the Institute of Contemporary Arts, London and the Bartlett School of Architecture at University College London. He has also curated the British Pavilion at the 9th Venice Architecture Biennale.

Mark Cousins is a cultural critic and architectural theorist. He is head of the Histories and Theories graduate programme at the AA. He has been visiting professor of architecture at Columbia University and is currently guest professor at South Eastern University in Nanjing. He is a founding member of the London Consortium.

Penelope Dean is an assistant professor at the University of Illinois at Chicago School of Architecture and founding editor of *Flat Out*, an architecture and design magazine emanating from America's Midwest. She is a former editor of the Berlage Institute's journal *hunch* (2003–07).

Odile Decq is the co-founder of ODBC, which won the golden lion at the 1996 Venice Architecture Biennale. She also teaches at the Ecole Spéciale d'Architecture, Paris.

Alexander Eisenschmidt is an architect and writer who teaches design and history and theory at the University of Illinois at Chicago School of Architecture and holds a visiting lecturer position at the University of Pennsylvania.

Sarah Entwistle researches on the theme of the architectural archive, focusing on the unrealised designs of Clive Entwistle. She has worked for Thomas Heatherwick Studio, Cazenove Architects and Charles Tashima Architecture. She has taught at the AA Summer School as unit tutor, and at the Dunamaise Arts Centre, masterclass tutor.

Eva Franch i Gilabert is the director of Storefront for Art and Architecture in New York and the founder of OOAA (office of architectural affairs). She is currently also teaching at Rice University as the Wortham Fellow.

Tony Fretton is the founder of Tony Fretton Architects. As well as being the principal designer of all projects, he is active in the discourse on design through lectures, seminars and writing.

Beatrice Galilee is a London-based curator, writer, critic, consultant and lecturer in contemporary architecture and design. She is the co-founder and director of The Gopher Hole, architectural consultant and writer at DomusWeb, as well as associate lecturer at Central St Martins.

Theaster Gates is an artist, urban planner and director of arts programming at the University of Chicago and is currently a Loeb Fellow at the Harvard Graduate School of Design. He exhibits internationally and was featured in the 2010 Whitney Biennial.

Sean Griffiths is a director and co-founder of FAT. He is a senior lecturer at the University of Westminster, the Louis I Kahn visiting professor of architecture at Yale School of Architecture and a contributor to CABE and RIBA.

Sarah Herda is the director of the Graham Foundation for Advanced Studies in the Fine Arts, and was previously director and curator of the Storefront for Art and Architecture. She also teaches at the University of Illinois at Chicago School of Architecture.

Florian Idenburg is the co-founder of SO-IL and teaches design studios at Harvard and Columbia. Previously he held the Brown-Forman Chair in Urban Design at the University of Kentucky, and was visiting lecturer at Princeton University.

Mary Jane Jacob is the executive director of exhibitions and a professor of sculpture at the School of the Art Institute of Chicago. She has formerly served as the chief curator of the MCA Chicago and MoCA Los Angeles.

Srdjan Jovanovic Weiss is the founder and chief designer of Normal Architecture Office. He is an assistant professor at Temple University, Tyler School of Art and has previously taught at Harvard GSD, UPenn, Columbia University, Parsons School of Design and Pratt Institute.

Lydia Kallipoliti is a practising architect, engineer and theorist. She is also assistant professor adjunct at the Irwin S Chanin School of Architecture at the Cooper Union in New York City.

Olympia Kazi is executive director of the Van Alen Institute at the Pratt Institute, and the former director of the Institute for Urban Design as well as Junior Curator at the Milan Triennale. She has been the architecture editor of *Wound* magazine and has written for *The Architect's Newspaper* and *Architectural Design*.

Prem Krishnamurthy is a principal of Project Projects, a design studio focusing on print, identity, exhibition and interactive work. The studio has been a finalist twice in the Cooper-Hewitt National Design Awards and has received numerous distinctions. The studio also produces independent curatorial and publishing projects.

Lisa Yun Lee is the director of the Jane Addams Hull-House Museum and a member of the Art History Faculty at the University of Illinois at Chicago. She is also the co-founder and former director of The Public Square at the Illinois Humanities Council.

Alex Lehnerer teaches at the University of Illinois at Chicago School of Architecture, where he serves as director of the Department of Urban Speculation. He is also a partner of Zurich-based firm Kaisersrot and a.l.s.o. Architekten.

Andres Lepik is the former curator of Architecture and Design at the Museum of Modern Art in New York. He is also the former chief curator of the Architectural Collection at Staatliche Museen zu Berlin and a widely published writer.

Aaron Levy is the executive director and chief curator at the Slought Foundation in Philadelphia. He also lectures in the departments of English and History of Art at the University of Pennsylvania. He recently published *Architecture on Display*, a research initiative and living history of the Venice Biennale of Architecture, with William Menking.

Ariane Lourie Harrison is a designer, educator and co-founder of Harrison Atelier. She has taught at the Yale School of Architecture since 2006. She is a LEED AP and directs the firm's practice in environmental design.

Scrap Marshall is the co-founder of the Public Occasion Agency (POA) an agency interested in the intersections of architecture, education, engagement and participation. He is currently finishing his diploma in architecture at the AA.

William Menking is the founder and editor in chief of *The Architect's Newspaper* as well as professor of Architecture, Urbanism and City Planning at the Pratt Institute. He recently published *Architecture on Display*, a research initiative and living history of the Venice Biennale of Architecture, with Aaron Levy.

Abaseh Mirvali is the executive director of the Colección/Fundación Jumex. She is also a member of the foundation Patronato de Arte Contemporáneo, A.C, and was formerly the special projects coordinator for Education and Bi-national Culture for the office of the United States Ambassador to Mexico.

Jan Nauta graduated from the AA Diploma School in 2011, winning the AA Prize. He is the co-founder of the Public Occasion Agency (with Scrap Marshall) and works as an architect, writer and organiser.

Vanessa Norwood is head of exhibitions at the AA, organising and curating architecture related shows and events. Previously she has worked for architects Lifschutz Davidson and de Rijke Marsh Morgan.

John Palmesino is an architect and urbanist. He has established Territorial Agency, an independent organisation that works for integrated spatial transformations. He is unit master at the AA School of Architecture and research advisor at the Jan van Eyck Academie in Maastricht.

Yael Reisner is an architectural designer, academic, researcher and writer. She is the director of Yael Reisner Studio, Architecture and Design. She teaches internationally at Sci Arc in LA, Lund University in Sweden and the AA in London.

Charles Renfro is a partner in Diller Scofidio + Renfro, an interdisciplinary design studio based in New York City. His adjunct faculty appointments have included Columbia University, Rice University and Parsons The New School for Design.

Kari Rittenbach is currently assistant curator at Barbican Art Gallery in London. She has written about art and architecture for *frieze*, *Paper Monument*, *032c*, *domusweb*, *PIN-UP*, The Bi Blog and others.

Ken Saylor is the co-founder of saylor + sirola, an NYC-based architecture, art and design consultancy. His work has been published in *Progressive Architecture*, *Interior Design*, *Metropolis*, *Artforum* and *The New York Times* and he has lectured and participated in numerous symposia across the country.

Ingrid Schroeder is a studio tutor at the AA and Cambridge University, where she also lectures on American Urban Theory. She is conducting PhD research at the LSE, a project that explores how the development of Washington DC serves to construct an idea of American citizenship.

Jason Schupbach is the design director for the National Endowment for the Arts. He has a background in public policy and urban planning and was previously the creative economy industry director for the Massachusetts Office of Business Development.

Shohei Shigematsu is currently director of the Office for Metropolitan Architecture in New York. He was the project leader for the winning entry for the CCTV headquarters in Beijing and has been involved in projects such as the Universal headquarters in Los Angeles, the Whitney Museum extension in NYC and the Tokyo vertical Campus.

Andre Singer is the co-founder of Project².

Brett Steele is the director of the Architectural Association School of Architecture and AA Publications. Brett is the founder and former director of the AADRL Design Research Lab and has taught and lectured at schools throughout the world.

Léa-Catherine Szacka is a PhD candidate at the Bartlett School of Architecture with a thesis on

'Exhibiting the Postmodern: Three Narratives for a History of the 1980 Venice Architecture Biennale'. In the past year she has collaborated with the Barbican in London and Centre Pompidou, Paris.

Tricia Van Eck is the founding director of communal art space 6018 North. She is a former associate curator at the MCA Chicago where she notably organised *Without You I'm Nothing: Art and Its Audience* (2010–11) and the ongoing performance series *Here/Not There*.

Nader Vossoughian is a curator, critic and theorist. Currently, he is a lecturer at the Museum of Modern Art and an assistant professor of architecture at the New York Institute of Technology.

Mark Wasiuta is the director of exhibitions at Columbia University's Graduate School of Architecture, Planning and Preservation where he is also on the faculty. Additionally, he is a co-founder and partner at the International House of Architecture (IHA).

Mark Wigley is the dean of Columbia University's Graduate School of Architecture, Planning and Preservation. He is also a founder of *Volume* magazine together with Rem Koolhaas and Ole Bouman.

Liam Young is a freelance architect and the founder of Tomorrow's Thought Today, a London-based think tank exploring the consequences of fantastic, perverse and underrated urbanisms. He has previously worked with Zaha Hadid and has been part of the faculty at the AA, Bartlett Architecture School, Cambridge University and Oxford Brookes University.

Michael Young is an architect and an educator practising in New York City. He is a co-founder of the architecture and urban design practice Young & Ayata.

Colophon

Four Conversations on the Architecture of Discourse
Aaron Levy and William Menking

Managing Editor: Thomas Weaver
Publications Editor: Pamela Johnston
Art Director: Zak Kyes
Design: Wayne Daly
Editorial Assistant: Clare Barrett

Titles set in Maria, designed by Phil Baber
Text set in Elzevir Book
Printed in Germany by
GGP Media GmbH, Pössneck

ISBN 978-1-907896-19-4

For a catalogue of AA Publications visit
www.aaschool.ac.uk/publications
or email publications@aaschool.ac.uk

AA Publications, 36 Bedford Square
London WC1B 3ES
T + 44 (0)20 7887 4021
F + 44 (0)20 7414 0783

SLOUGHT
FOUNDATION